1000

Racing Quotations

1000
Racing Quotations

Graham Sharpe

A Racing Post company

Published in 2007 by Highdown,
an imprint of Raceform Ltd
Compton, Newbury, Berkshire, RG20 6NL

A catalogue record for this book is available from the British Library.

ISBN 978-1-905156-33-7

Cover designed by Tracey Scarlett
Interiors designed by Adrian Morrish

Printed in Great Britain by William Clowes Ltd, Beccles, Suffolk

INTRODUCTION

The most famous and enduring quote in racing is, I believe, 'Eclipse first, the rest nowhere', uttered as long ago as 3 May 1769 when the legendary champion of that name contested a race at Epsom where his professional gambler owner, the colourful Captain Dennis O'Kelly, used the phrase to strike a bet indicating that his runner would win so easily that those labouring in his wake would be so far behind that they would not be officially placed.

The bold bet was landed, the confident phrase duly recorded and it entered the folklore of the sport. But was it an accurate quote? I have recently come across evidence which suggests that what was actually said may have been subtly different.

Respected turf historian, James Christie Whyte, writing in 1840 when Eclipse, winner of all 21 of his starts, and O'Kelly were still recalled at first hand by some ancient racing folk, explained that 'all the best six-years-old horses of the year having entered against Eclipse for the King's Plate, O'Kelly offered to take ten to one, he posted them, which being bettered to an immense amount, and the captain called upon to declare, he pronounced, "Eclipse! and nothing else" – implying the rest to be "nowhere", which was really the case, for the rider of Eclipse, having received private instructions to go off at score, double distanced the whole with the greatest ease, leaving himself without a competitor'.

But regardless of the actual words uttered, there is little doubt that the impact of a pivotal moment in racing history echoes down the years to this day because of this striking phrase which captures perfectly the essence of a great horse's domination of its era.

Whilst researching the archives for this compilation I also came across an alternative version of another classic quote. Scottish bookie John Banks is infamous for his description of betting shops as being 'a licence to print money.' But I have found reference to him actually saying: 'I don't call them betting shops. I call them money factories. To have one is a licence to steal money.' A subtle difference, but significant.

Rather like legendary Liverpool soccer manager Bill Shankly's remark about football being more important than life itself, whatever the actual form of words used at the time, it is the sense and symbolism of pithy, memorable remarks which imprint themselves on the public consciousness and warrants their retention and recording as iconic, informative summations of essential truths.

What I have endeavoured to do in this latest collection of quotes from hundreds of years of racing is to chronicle comments, quips and considerations of the sport's past, present and future which are worth compiling for their insight, impact, humour, controversy and contribution to the greater appreciation of the multi-faceted Sport of Kings.

Graham Sharpe

****

'You made me look a **** once, I'm not a **** twice' ... Mick Easterby's rapid fire double use of the dreaded c-word, caused uproar during an interview with Alistair Down on Channel 4 on 17 May 2006. The Channel was forced to apologise on his behalf. Easterby's own explanation for using the word was something of a collector's item: 'It is a slang word in Yorkshire, that comes from the Anglo-Saxons and it has been translated into a swear word. It's an old Yorkshire expression that means 'silly b*gger' but if anyone was offended then I am deeply sorry. I have a friend and I've called him that every day of my life' ... mm, I believe you, Mick. Paul Haigh joined in the controversy in the *Racing Post* a day or two later: 'Some of the worst people never swear, at least in public. Some of the best never stop. So why the apologies when a man speaks as he'd happily speak at home?' – I don't f***ing know Haigh, you ****.

A?
'Our sincere apologies to all those Express Racing followers who called in yesterday – and to all who suffered in silence. The letter 'A' did not appear in the names of horses in the racecards. This was due to a computer error' ... *Daily Express, 6 December 1996*

ABILITY
'Ability does not get you a glass of water in racing. It is not what you know, but who you know' ... Paul Kelleway, 1996.

ABROAD

'The black population is invisible' ... Julian Wilson on racing in South Africa. *Racing Post, 10 March 2005*

'While there are more than 40 licensed tracks, only six are operational on anything other than an irregular basis; many are not functioning at all at the moment.' ... Nicholas Godfrey on racing in Brazil. *Racing Post, 7 August 2005*

ABSENCE OF WOMEN

'A few high profile trainers and even fewer jockeys at the top level cannot conceal the absence of women at the sharp end of the sport' ... authors Wray Vamplew and Joyce Kay pointing out an unpalatable, but undeniable truth in their 2005 *Encyclopaedia of British Horseracing*, adding gloomily, 'the future for most women in racing does not seem appreciably brighter at the beginning of the twenty first century than it did twenty years earlier.'

ABSURD

'An occasion when racing's most affluent and powerful gather to spend absurd amounts on unproven young horseflesh' ... Richard Edmondson on Newmarket's Tattersalls October Sale. *The Independent, 4 October 2005*

'The idea that they are unaware of horses not run on their merits for financial gain with the complicity of at least the jockey, if not always the trainer and/or owner, is utterly absurd' ... *Times* racing writer Lydia Hislop is unimpressed with jockeys Kevin Darley and the Hills twins, Michael and Richard who insisted in a 2006 letter to the *Racing Post* that 'there is no fixing of races'.

ABUSE
'From 1989 through 2004 – from Patrick Valenzuela to the late Chris Antley to Pat Day to Jerry Bailey to Jose Santos to Stewart Elliott – at least half of the Kentucky Derbies were won by riders with documented or admitted substance-abuse problems at some point in their professional careers' ... Pat Forde, *allhorseracing.com, 3 March 2006*

ACCIDENT
'With the increase of both traffic congestion and racing fixtures, it's just a matter of time until a serious road accident occurs which, apart from the seriousness to those involved, will bring racing unwanted publicity' ... Tony Culhane explains why a majority of jockeys voted for a rule restricting them to one meeting per day. *Racing Post, 4 June 2006*

ACHIEVEMENT
'Mine's up there now, twice. It's not the feeling you've achieved something, it's that you're actually there, part of it all. It's overwhelming' ... Mick Fitzgerald marvels at being one of the jockeys whose peg in the Cheltenham changing room records his name and big race triumphs there.

'It's a fantastic achievement for an operation that started off with just four horses and now has horses all over the world' … perhaps he would say that, wouldn't he? Frankie Dettori in October 2005 as Godolphin notched its 1,000th winner – the Frankie-ridden Highlander at Nottingham.

ACTING
'It took me forever to understand what acting was really about. I was too busy thinking of other things – horses and gambling, bridge and lovemaking' … Omar Sharif, seemingly getting his priorities right. *Night & Day, 10 July 2005*

'Jenny Pitman' … John Francome's answer to the question, 'Favourite Actress'. He also answered 'Gynaecologist' to 'Alternative Career'. *Sportsman, 29 May 2006*

ADDICTION
'If you're compulsive obsessive it's giving a great addiction, and once you're hooked on it it's hard to get out' … John Gosden, on the pull of training to its practitioners. *Channel 4 interview with Alice Plunkett, 28 May 2005*

ADDRESS
'Desert Orchid, Somewhere in England' … address on Christmas card from Australia – which arrived safely. Henrietta Knight also reported similar mail sent to 'Best Mate, Oxfordshire'.

ADORED
'He adored the sport, the horses, the people and the game itself'
… Nicky Henderson pays tribute to David 'The Duke' Nicholson, who died in August 2006.

ADULATION
'The commonest jockey boy in this company of manikins can usually earn more than the average scholar or professional man, and the whole set receive a good deal more of adulation than has been bestowed on any soldier, sailor, explorer or scientific man of our generation' … J Runciman in his April 1889 article, 'The Ethics of the Turf'.

ADVANTAGE
'Everyone in racing knows that horses have – to put it another, more palatable way – 'quiet runs'. And not only do we – owners, trainers, jockeys, stable staff, journalists – put up with it. We all try and use it to our own advantage' … 'Newsboy', the *Daily Mirror* racing columnist, points out one of racing's great hypocrisies.

ADVERT
'Call that an advert? I could do better with my knob and a pot of paint' … the late, eponymous William Hill, a man who, as you will have detected, did not suffer fools gladly, on being presented with some advertising ideas by 'creatives'. *Iain Murray, Marketing Week, 25 June 2006*

ADVICE

'Come back when you're not pregnant' ... useful advice from his Bajan water-skiing instructor to a portly Richard Pitman.

AFRAID

'I know how to train, I know when I have a good one and I know what to do with them. I'm not afraid of anything – not even when I'm lying on the ground getting kicked!' ... irrepressible veteran handler Clive Brittain. *Racing Post, 13 July 2006*

AGEING

'He's improved as he's got older. I thought I might do the same, but it hasn't happened!' ... trainer Milton Bradley on his May 2005 Haydock winner, eight-year-old sprinter Corridor Creeper.

AGENTS

'Perhaps his slump in fortune was linked to a bizarre tendency to switch agents at the drop of a hat' ... Rodney Masters considers Darryl Holland's disappointing 2005 season. *Racing Post, 29 December 2005*

AGGRESSION

'Entering the grandstand was like walking into a low-rent nightclub, full of aggression towards both men and (in a sexual way) women' ... *Racing Post*, reader Jane Osbourne complains in the paper about the atmosphere at Newmarket for the 2006 2000 guineas.

A.I.
'Artificial insemination is a crazy idea. Who wants 100 Mill Reefs anyway?' ... Richard Baerlein, racing writer of *The Observer*, 1978.

AIRPORT
'It looks like Munich Airport – and I don't like Munich Airport' ... 70-year-old racegoer Colin Sheppard – on a flying visit, perhaps – on the new Ascot grandstand. *The Times, 21 June 2006*

ALCOHOL
'Without claiming to be any authority on the subject I think that the effect of alcohol on a jockey is to make him think that he is riding better than he actually appears to the spectator, and that when he feels the need to avail himself of Dutch Courage he should retire, before an over-generous dose brings about an interview with the stewards' ... advice as sage today as it was when issued in 1951 by John Hislop and John Skeaping in their book, *Steeplechasing*.

ALERT
'Because it might alert the animal activists unnecessarily, I'm told' ... Howard Wright reveals why the HRA refuses to permit whip offences revealed in stewards inquiries, being relayed to the crowd via the PA system or on the HRA website. 'That's not a good enough reason to keep basic information away from the race-going public,' complained Wright. *Racing Post, 4 August 2006*

ALL SINGING AND ...

'We don't expect him to come out singing and dancing after such a lengthy absence' ... the Queen's racing manager, John Warren, indicating that her horse Promotion might have some unexpected talents to reveal in the fullness of time. *Racing Post, 30 April 2005*

'(Nick) Atkinson once won £250 on a flutter and decided to name his band in honour of the hoofed hero' ... how singer Nick Atkinson's winning punt on Champion Hurdler Rooster Booster resulted in his chart-busting band becoming 'Rooster'. *The Eye, 30 April 2005*

ALTERNATIVE

'My ally is Charlotte Watt, an MS sufferer from Edinburgh, who never sees the horses. She's a Reiki healer who seems to have a strange understanding of how horses work' ... trainer Paul Keane might be onto something as Ms Watt suggested in 2005 that his Bill Owen would benefit from wearing blinkers rather than cheek-pieces – and he promptly won at Taunton.

AMBITION

'If you said to me, would you rather win this or train a horse to win the Derby, you know, I'd rather win this' ... flat trainer Sir Mark Prescott, quizzed by journalist Peter Oborne, admitted that the Derby played second string in his mind to coursing's Waterloo Cup. *The Spectator, 19 February 2005*

AMBITIOUS

'I can't see the point of it, if you're not winning. I can't help the way I am. I'm the world's worst loser, ultra-ambitious, and I have no fear when it comes to taking on the big boys' ... rookie trainer David Flood. *Racing Post, 12 June 2005*

AMERICA

'I don't understand how a man who can train the first five home in the (Cheltenham) Gold Cup can waste his time pissing about with Flat horses in America' ... Ginger McCain articulates what many have feared to utter as Michael Dickinson wins the *Racing Post 100 Greatest Training Feats* accolade in March 2006.

ANGEL

'Now but very little lower than the angels' ... opinion of late 19th century racing writer William Black on the then status of trainers – and one no doubt shared by a number of that profession today. Another writer from that generation, W A C Blew wrote in 1900, 'the house of a well-to-do trainer is far superior in its decorations and adornments to the house of many a country gentleman ... one or two we could mention have, or have had, footmen in livery behind their chairs.'

ANORAK?

'The Melbourne Cup is only a long-distance handicap and should be referred to by its correct name – the Australian Cesarewitch' ... what fun it must be to be racing historian John Randall, who wrote of Makybe Diva's record breaking, November 2005, third consecutive 'Melbourne Cup' victory that the mare's degree of greatness 'depends on the quality of her performances, not on the number of times she has been favoured by the weights.' Lighten up, man!

ANSWER

'Horses don't answer back' ... Mick Channon, asked by writer Tony Rushmer why he opted for racehorse training over football management. *FourFourTwo magazine, September 2006*

APOLOGETIC

'With the start of the British flat season, you get two thirds of bugger all and an apologetic shrug' ... Peter Thomas. *Racing Post, 27 March 2006*

ARCHITECT

'The architect had never done a grandstand before. But he had done a lot of churches' ... so, no change there, then! Lord Hesketh on the newly erected grandstand at Huntingdon where he pioneered free entry. *Daily Telegraph, 3 November 2005*

ARGY BARGY

'The meeting starts at 2.30pm and still isn't finished eight and a half hours later at 11pm under floodlights' ... *Racing Post* writer Nicholas Godfrey's stamina is tested at Buenos Aires' track, Palermo, where there were 16 races on the card in August 2005.

ARISTOCRACY
'The course will be the nearest to France, and large numbers of the French aristocracy will be attracted to meetings' ... rash prediction from the *Folkestone Herald* in 1896 when plans were announced for the new Folkestone racecourse.

ARSE
'Nothing just comes. If you go out and work really, really hard – harder than the competition – it's amazing what you can make happen. But if you just sit on your arse expecting it all to come to you, it won't' ... journeyman jockey turned controversial trainer, David Flood, who declared: 'I couldn't give a shit how I'm perceived by other trainers'. *Racing Post, 8 June 2005*

'It gets you out of the home, but you can't kick the trousers off a bare ass' ... now, this is only my theory, but could bookmaker Kevin McManus, brother of J.P., have been bemoaning the strength of the market at Clonmel in March 2006?

'I saw the arse end coming over and if I hadn't got my head clear by inches that would have been it' ... trainer George Margarson on the fall he took at Bangor after which a somersaulting horse nearly ended his life, let alone his career. *The Spectator, 15 June 2006*

'What we do is very inexact, and horses can make an arse of you' ... Sir Michael Stoute.

ART
'Bollocks' ... title of limited edition print by artist Chris Howells, depicting a dejected jockey sitting on the floor, following a fall.

'The "art" is created by horses using their noses, lips and tails' ... American thoroughbred rehabilitation organisation ReRun Inc sells 'Moneigh' paintings created by big name equine stars like Cigar, Smarty Jones and Funny Cide who use paintbrushes! *Racing Post, 14 December 2005*

ARTIFICIAL INSEMINATION
'Suppose bottles of Hyperion or Fairway extract were disseminated all over the world; with hundreds and hundreds of mares in foal to these two horses, in the course of a year or two your breed would be so inbred that it would deteriorate beyond all imagination' ... president of the Thoroughbred Breeders Association, the Earl of Rosebery, discussing artificial insemination in his 1945 address to the AGM.

ASHES TO ASHES
'Rod (Fabricius, managing director of the course) and I had a chat and it was decided, with collective wisdom, to scatter Persian Punch's ashes at Goodwood. It was a very private affair. We went over one evening and did what was necessary' ... owner Jeff Smith, whose great public favourite is commemorated by a green slate plaque at Goodwood. *The Times, 26 July 2005*

ASTROLOGY

'Improving performance: includes visit to assess horse and astrological analysis – £486' ... price-sheet for unusual service offered to those wishing to identify possible equine performance potential, by former silversmith and publisher, John Puxty. *The Times, 9 February 2006*

'There is no royal road to success in breeding, wither by the aid of Astrology, Botany or Physiology, but these all have their use if applied in an intelligent manner' ... some may choose, churlishly in my opinion, to disagree with this statement by unconventional late 19th/early 20th century breeder, Colonel William Hall-Walker, which he made in 1908.

ATHLETE

'A horse must have rhythm. He has to move like an athlete. Also, I never knew a good racehorse that didn't have a good head. I have a preference for small eyes and small ears' ... and Sir Michael Stoute should know. *The Observer, 30 July 2006*

'No athletic enclave in America is home to more reclamation projects – physical, mental, emotional – than the jocks' room. Even at the high end of the sport' ... *Pat Forde, allhorseracing.com, 3 May 2006*

ATTENTION

'With the modern film star, you don't actually feel that owning a

winning horse would be a pleasure; you feel, instead, that they would resent the attention being taken away from them' ... Laura Thompson bemoans the passing of the days when Judy Garland, Liz Taylor, Frank Sinatra, Bing Crosby, Cary Grant et al were keen owners. *Pacemaker, June 1999*

AT THE END OF THE DAY
'The Bula title has had its day. There will be a large number of today's generation of racegoers who would not even have seen Bula run' ... Cheltenham director of sponsorship Peter McNeile in October 2006, justifying changing a race name commemorating one of the sport's all time greats, the Bula Hurdle, to the Boylesports.com International. So, I suppose no one not around when the Beatles were a band wants to listen to their music today?

AUCTION
'Race due to start at 4pm. Sponsorship will include entry to the course, naming rights to race title, which will be used in press and advanced publicity and PA announcements before and after the race' ... Ayr racecourse put up a 2m 6f handicap hurdle to be run on April 16, 2005, for auction on eBay in March 2005.

'Norman is now hanging above my bed for the time being and I'm very pleased with him' ... former trainer Charlie Books, who splashed out £220.90 to acquire the 'Norman Williamson' jockey's board from Ascot in an auction of that course's assets in May 2005 whilst refurbishment work was ongoing.

'It reads "Well done from mere mortal jocks". Then there is another word that someone has attempted to blank out. It appears to start with a "w" and end with an "r"...' ... Charlie Brooks on the inscription penned by Pat Eddery on Frankie Dettori's Ascot weighing room saddle rack after his historic Magnificent Seven at the track, which fetched £2,000 in an auction (sold to Frankie's agent, Pete Burrell).

AWFUL

'The five furlong track at Liverpool was bloody awful because they were coming straight at you and you couldn't tell who had won' ... clerk of the course at Aintree, John Hughes, in 1975 after flat racing was dropped by the track.

BACKFLIP

'I was scared and I hang on real good when I'm scared. And Alex, he's so athletic I think he could do a backflip if you asked him to' ... jockey Jeremy Rose explains how he managed to stay aboard Afleet Alex as the horse nearly crashed to the ground after clashing with Scrappy T during the 2005 Preakness Stakes only to recover and go on to win.

BAD RACING

'Much as I love racing, I love variety more. I had to turn down a posting on one of the racing channels, because bad racing has never interested me ... against the more routine race meetings I find an Olympic Games a far greater source of excitement' ... Clare Balding. *Daily Telegraph, 29 September 2006*

BAG

'Amateur rider Stephen Davis produced from his pocket a yellow plastic bag. He proceeded to complete the course carrying the bag, which he occasionally waved at his mount (Arcticflow) who was tailed off from halfway' … Richard Hoiles explains why the stewards at Hereford on 8 April 1995 fined Davis £75.

BAIL

'Perhaps a contest between jockeys who are on bail against those who aren't would sell' … Sir Clement Freud offers an alternative format to the organisers of the Shergar Cup. *Racing Post, 16 August 2006*

BALLS

'It was reported that he had injured his testicles when whipping round on the way to the start' … Robert Carter, on unusual injury for 2004 Derby Italiano winner, Groom Tesse.

BALLS UP

'When I started out in this job I was told that every time you climb on the rostrum you're only two seconds away from a balls-up' … ex-jockey turned Cheltenham Festival starter, Peter Haynes. *Racing Post, 3 March 2005*

'I am so lucky to have this horse and not to have made a balls-up of it all' … modesty from Derby winning trainer Michael Bell, after Motivator won the 2005 Blue Riband.

'I have made the biggest balls-up since I started training and I have apologised to Mr Hemmings. I said I should never have run him' ... what's this – a trainer not only admitting to a mistake, but apologising for it! Nicky Richards is self-critical after running his owner's well thought of Turpin Green to finish only 3rd at Kelso, having won ten days earlier.

BANDAGES
'I don't bandage - bandaging is a considerable skill and done badly it can cause more problems than it solves' ... Jamie Osborne. *Spectator, 18 August 2007*

BARTER SYSTEM
'Bartering is a fascinating and exciting idea and I can't see any reason why it wouldn't work in a racing context' ... Charlie Mann became the first British trainer to sell a horse for an equivalent value under a bartering system all the rage in Australia when, reportedly in September 2005, David Wilson, chief executive of company Bartercard, purchased a four year old from him for the equivalent of £25,000 which Mann could 'spend' on services from other companies tied in to the scheme. *Racing Post, 4 September 2005*

BA*TARDS
'I've been astounded how open doors have been – after all I've been away a while. I never realised until now I was such a popular ba*tard' ... the irrepressible trainer Rod Simpson. *The Sportsman, 29 August 2006*

'They'll have to find some other ba*tard, won't they?' ... David 'The Duke' Nicholson retiring immediately after winning on What A Buck at Hereford in 1974, only to be reminded by the clerk of the scales that he had a mount in the next race. Geoff Lester remembering an encounter with the jockey–turned-trainer, who died in August 2006. *The Sportsman, 29 August 2006*

'I'm not a fanny merchant. If a horse is a ba*tard, I say so' ... Paul Kelleway, 1969.

'When I was a jockey I was a hungry little ba*tard, and I'm still the same hungry little ba*tard' ... trainer David Bridgwater who broke a 512 day drought when Country Affair won at Newton Abbot in August 2007.

BEADS
'Men walked round offering the girls beads to take their clothes off. Many were only too happy to oblige' ... one of the Kentucky Derby traditions they don't tell you about in the tourist brochures. *Andy Lines, The Sportsman, 8 May 2006*

BEAR NECESSITY
'He had with him his great black bear and, for spite at being beaten, he took off its muzzle. Right toward the people it ran, and soon cleared the field of all spectators' ... the 1824 Lancashire 'Borough Record' reports how an owner reacted when his horse was defeated at the now defunct Clitheroe racecourse.

BEATEN

'**We were beaten by a better horse and a nicer trainer**' ... gallant Sir Mark Prescott on Pam Sly whose Speciosa had just seen off his Confidential Lady in the 2006 1000 Guineas.

BEAUTIFUL

'**The most beautiful scenery in the world is in England, so beautiful, so green, you feel like you are in heaven when you see the rivers and the countryside. Perfect**' ... Godolphin trainer Saeed Bin Suroor turns into an Anglophile in July 2005.

BED

'**Look at that power and movement and muscle. It reminds me of me in bed**' ... Henrietta Knight was making no comment after this boast by partner Terry Biddlecombe was made as he admired Philip Blacker's Cheltenham statue of Best Mate in March 2006.

BEST

'**I haven't the slightest interest in being champion trainer. I would like to be the best trainer, though I don't know what that is**' ... Sir Mark Prescott, who is just champion in many people's eyes. *Pacemaker, July 2005*

'**No getting away from that imperious exhibition of 40 Octobers ago as the very best of the best in the annals of racing**' ... Tony Morris on Sea Bird's 1965 Arc triumph. (*Pacemaker, October 2005*). Oddly, in the very same edition, James Willoughby disagreed:

'the single greatest performance in thoroughbred history on 9 June 1973,' he declared, referring to Secretariat's Belmont Stakes victory by 31 lengths.

'Statistics say that Sir Gordon (Richards) was the best. But I always thought Lester was the best and Scobie (Breasley) was just behind him' ... and not far behind them all was Mill Reef's jockey, Geoff Lewis. *Racing Post, 28 May 2006*

'He's the best horse I've ever trained. He may be the best horse anyone has ever trained' ... Bill Mott on his US Champion, Cigar.

'I'm not convinced that he is even the best jockey riding at present' ... Julian Wilson on Kieren Fallon. *Racing Post, 25 July 2006*

'You can be the best jockey in the world, but if you don't have the horses it's hard to ride winners' ... 39-year-old Irish jockey Kevin Manning on his lengthy career. *The Sportsman, 6 August 2006*

BEST LAID PLANS ...
'We were not having a good day, so Kevin (Keegan), Mick (Channon) and I pooled our money and gave it to Channon and the money was down. The horse romped in with us screaming it home. We couldn't wait to collect our winnings ... Then we saw a downcast Channon lumbering towards us. He had put the money on the wrong horse' ... the late 1966 England World Cup hero Alan Ball on a day at the races in New York 1981.

BEST MATE

'It was a great life, and in a way, a great death. A life worth celebrating, a death worth grieving for' ... Simon Barnes of *The Times*, on the death of Best Mate in a race at Exeter on 1 November 2005.

'I haven't cried because it was a good way for him to go' ... Terry Biddlecombe, husband of the horse's trainer, Henrietta Knight.

'A few minutes ago I was leaning over the rail watching him in the parade, thinking "you're the most beautiful horse ever created" ... Horses have to go. We all have to go.' Henrietta Knight

'He'll be up there in the sky now taking on Arkle – and he'll probably beat him' ... owner Jim Lewis. He can have 10/1 with me!

'I wonder if the thought has stolen across their minds, as it did across mine, that after three Gold Cup wins and a burst blood vessel, should they not have retired him? What more was it reasonable to expect the poor beast to achieve?' ... David Mellor is not sympathetic towards Hen and Terry. *Evening Standard, 4 November 2005*

'They say only pets can be buried, but I loved Best Mate more than any pet' ... Jim Lewis on the Euro law which prevented him burying Best Mate where he collapsed and died at Exeter and meant the horse would have to be cremated. Pets are exempt. *The Sun, 3 November 2005*

'I remember looking into his eye just before he died; he was very calm and peaceful' ... Best Mate's groom, Jackie Jenner. *Racing Ahead, December 2005*

'The more we concrete over the world, the more horses such as Best Mate mean to people' ... Simon Barnes. *The Times, 4 November 2005*

'Instead of feeling sorry for Best Mate and those other legends of the horse racing world, we should look on the positive side and be warmed by our memories of the times we shared with these wonderful and noble creatures' ... Jenny Pitman. *Daily Mail, 3 November 2005*

'Peter Brookes is an experienced and award-winning cartoonist and he pulls no punches in his work. His cartoon is one part of a mosaic of opinion pieces in the Comment Pages. Mr Brookes daily tackles difficult subjects in contemporary affairs, and his interpretations are not always to everyone's taste' ... *The Times* 'Feedback' column 'apologising unreservedly' to readers 'inadvertently' offended by a cartoon published shortly after Best Mate's death and David Blunkett's resignation from the Cabinet, showing Tony Blair in jockey silks riding a horse with David Blunkett's head, splayed out on all fours as though he had just fallen. It was captioned 'Best Mate'. *The Times, 5 November 2005*

'The funny thing about that was that all the letters of complaint were from racegoers and race people, mainly from Newmarket. Not one complaint was concerned that I had depicted Blunkett in an unflattering light' ... cartoonist Brookes. Not sure I believe the 'Newmarket' bit, though. *The Independent, 6 January 2006*

'Best Mate was a horse. Get over it' ... Des Kelly is unsympathetic. *Daily Mail, 8 November 2005*

'In terms of price, Best Mate was worth a fraction of his Flat-racing colleagues. As for real value, his worth was beyond figures' ... Clare Balding. *The Observer, 6 November 2005*

BET
'I love horse racing. I don't bet on cricket, tennis, golf, football. Just the horses. My first bet would have been nearly forty years ago at Caymanas Park in Jamaica' ... feared West Indian fast bowler Michael Holding. *The Sportsman, 15 August 2006*

'You're better off betting on a horse than betting on a man. A horse may not be able to hold you tight, but he doesn't wanna wander from the stable at night' ... actress Betty Grable.

BETTER
'I don't think there's anything about racing that is better now than when I started' ... trainer Barry Hills. *Pacemaker, June 2006*

BETTING

'I won £54,000 on a bet, and I've lost £30,000 on a single bet. It would have been on the horses. But I don't bet now, I don't enjoy it' ... former Arsenal and England footballer Paul Merson. *FourFourTwo, November 2006*

'A trip to a football ground is already remarkably like entering a High Street betting shop' ... try as I might I can't quite work out what Paul Hayward was getting at in his *Daily Telegraph* column in February 2005. He was a little concerned about the link between sport and gambling which, he feels, 'are on their way to becoming indivisible. Forget Lost Wages. The biggest game in town is Lost Integrity.'

'That was quite painful and we've lost employees already as a result' ... Betfair's legal counsel David O'Reilly reveals that the exchange now forbids employees to bet. *BOS magazine, 2005*

'Freud and each-way are not words that are compatible' ... Sir Clement is a win-only man. *Racing Post, 23 March 2005*

'If you mind losing more than you enjoy winning, do not bet' ... Sir Clement Freud. *Racing Post, 14 June 2006*

'People who have never risked anything on a horse – and lost, and cursed – and gone back to the boards to bet on the next race – will never understand what makes the sport so fascinating, so thrilling' ... Ken Jones. *The Independent, 18 March 2005*

'I've never had a bet in my life. Even if I was offered 1000/1 about a horse I knew was a probable winner, I wouldn't chance 50p' ... church-going, teetotal trainer Peter Bowen. *News of the World, 3 April 2005*

'I remember it clearly. The shop with its sawdust floor and the butcher with his straw hat' ... Sir Peter O'Sullevan recalling his first Grand National bet – 6d (2 1/2p) each-way on 1928's 100/1 winner, Tipperary Tim, struck, pre-betting shops, with the local butcher. *The Independent, 4 April 2005*

'Universal recognition that betting is the overwhelming driver for British racing has been a long time coming. It's here now but so too should be the acceptance that the betting industry no longer owes the sport a living' ... Howard Wright. *Racing Post, 21 October 2005*

'I was betting an average of about $80,000 a race. It's quite a bit when you don't know the names of the horses' ... Starcraft's flamboyant owner Paul Makin, on how he used to gamble profitably on the Hong Kong and Japanese totes using a computer system. October 2005

'It was really all guesswork – there was no intelligence or science involved. I only go racing about once a year and bet about £5 a race' ... which explains how Ian Humphreys came to win the Tote Jackpot for £124,777.80 in November 2005, I suppose.

'I will happily confirm that I love the buzz from backing a winner' ... England striker Michael Owen. *The Times, 16 January 2006*

'If you win a race you're happy, if you lose you're depressed, a bet either way won't change that' ... owner David Sullivan. *Racing Post, 18 June 2006*

'If betting were done away with, there would be very few noblemen or gentlemen found willing and many unable to keep and run racehorses' ... the anonymous author of 1863's *Horse Racing; It's History and Early Records* admits what is rarely accepted even today.

'Run them where you like and when you think best only let me know when they are worth backing or that you have backed them for me' ... instructions many handlers might like to hear today, issued to trainer William Day (and recalled by him in his 1886 memoirs, *Reminiscences of the Turf*) by owner Lord Palmerston.

'A necessary adjunct to racing' ... dictator of the Turf, Admiral Rous, with a realistic view of betting's relationship with the Sport of Kings, in 1856.

'She was famed for betting, boozing and hats' ... and owning horses, of course – writer Richard Morrison remembers the Queen Mum. *The Knowledge, July 2006*

'I do not have space in mind to think about betting' … just as well – Japanese trainer Kojiro Hashiguchi's Heart's Cry was beaten when he brought him over for a crack at the 2006 King George at Ascot.

'It's the quiet bets that make the bookmakers noisy' … and with a name like that, 1945 racing writer John Betts should know.

'Other sports HAVE betting but racing in Britain NEEDS betting. It is because of this close connection that there is widespread perception of the sport as corrupt' … Wray Vamplew and Joyce Kay in the introduction to their 2005 *Encyclopaedia of British Horseracing*.

'Betting is the manure to which the enormous crop of horse racing and racehorse breeding in this and other countries is to a large extent due.' … R Black. *The Jockey Club and its Founders, 1891*

BETTING SHOPS
'In the past elderly people used to meet up in church to spend time with one another and organise such things as tea parties or coach trips to somewhere nice. Now they gather in betting shops' … young whipper-snapper Steve Palmer, who also remarked in passing, 'Only a pervert goes into a betting shop and doesn't bet his balls off.' *Racing Post, 23 July 2005*

'They let you into public houses for free as well, and you are guaranteed to leave them a lot happier than when you entered.

The same can't be said of betting shops, I'm afraid' ... Steve Palmer. *Racing Post, 23 July 2005*

'Betting shops are where you pay money to guess wrong' ... columnist Guy Browning. *Guardian Weekend, 6 August 2005*

'Dressed in striped pyjamas, he would stand in the corner and urinate on the floor before leaving with a cheery, "Goodbye, see you all soon"' ... Barry Dugard from Witney, Oxon, recalls the patron, 'an inmate from the local asylum', who would pay a weekly visit to his local betting shop back in the 1960s. *Racing Post, 19 September 2005*

'You can have a doctor and a loo cleaner patting each other on the back, one bloke's got £100 on it and one's got 50p, but for that moment they're united in slagging off a jockey or celebrating a goal. That's what you don't get sitting at a computer' ... Betting Shop Manager of the Year, Shaun Holden, on the enduring appeal of betting shops. *Racing Post, 20 July 2006*

'I wonder if gamblers are people who don't take their chances in the real world? I have gambled much more in the betting shop than in life' ... Andrew 'Bert' Black, one of the founders of Betfair. *Telegraph Magazine, 2006*

'Every time I enter a betting shop I am struck by the latent anger and vicious blame culture that accompanies the torn-up tickets

from yet another losing bet by one of those to whom this shop is the centre of daily life' … Alan Lee. *The Times, 23 September 2006*

BEYOND THE GRAVE?
'I went to my mother's grave and I said 'Mother, we need some rain', and I can't believe the rain she sent us' … owner of Iris's Gift, Robert Lester, attributes the mudlark's October 2005 win at Bangor to supernatural forces, a result which prompted *Racing Post* tipster Matt Williams to declare: 'I'll go and muck out 30 horses a day for a week at Jonjo O'Neill's yard if his horse wins the Gold Cup.'

BICYCLE CLIPS
'I had to put my bicycle clips on to stop the runs going from my rear into my shoes' … charming description of his feelings by Barry Dennis after taking a bet of £80,000 at 6/4 from J. P. McManus on his Baracouda for Cheltenham's 2005 World Hurdle, in which the horse was beaten. *talkSPORT, 18 August 2006*

BIRD
'She's some bird and just different class and she nicked that one' … trainer Enda Bolger on Nina Carberry after she won on Good Steo in Punchestown's La Touche Cup which he was winning for the 9th successive year in April 2006.

BIRD BRAINED
'One of the ostriches we've got is a bit "tup" as we call it in Wales

– a bit silly – and when we've got him turned out, she follows him around the field holding on to his tail. He doesn't seem to mind' ... owner Robert Bailey on York July 2005 winner Currency's unusual friend.

BIRTHPLACE
'England is the birthplace of the sport, so to go over there and ride big winners is very special. The public in England are the real fans of horseracing and of the horses themselves' ... see, someone loves us! French jockey Christophe Lemaire. *Racing Post, 23 July 2006*

BLEAK
'It's just too bleak there; the surface is too deep and the kickback too severe' ... Kieren Fallon is no fan of Southwell, to judge by this critical November 2005 description of the place.

BLEEDERS
'I reckon that in any race, half the horses are hurting and a third of them are bleeders' ... most of the ones I back, are. Welsh-based trainer Peter Bowen. *Sunday Telegraph, 22 October 2006*

BLINKERED VIEW
'He finished 13th and wore a pair of blinkers which I now think should be banned in that race. They are too dangerous on loose horses' ... Henrietta Knight, whose first Grand National runner, What's The Crack in 1992, wore the eye covers. *Observer Sports Monthly, March 2005*

'We're too blinkered to see it as a fantastic tasting meat' ... Janet Street Porter, who sold horse meat to Cheltenham racegoers at the 2007 Festival. Police accused her of being 'provocative' and moved her on.

BOARING
'Wild boars have ravaged the tiny racecourse at Gabarret in south-west France' ... *Racing Post* writer Graham Green reveals why racing was cancelled in May 2005 at a little known French track.

BOGGED DOWN
'How would he like it if the door to the lavatory suddenly opened while he was ensconced on the can, and someone with a big grin and a foolish chuckle enquired of him how things were going, were conditions underneath a bit on the firm side and could they mar his chances of success' ... *Racing Post* correspondent Tony Verdie complains about Derek Thompson's Channel 4 interviews with jockeys prior to, and immediately after, races. *Racing Post, 10 July 2005*

BOLLOCKING
'That's another daft jockey I've got. He knew he was in for a bollocking if it went wrong, but he rode a great race' ... Martin Pipe forgives Tom Malone for ignoring orders by front-running on Cheltenham winner Cantgeton on 26 October 2005.

'Few could give a jockey such a bollocking, but none was as loyal

to their man when others sought to criticise him' ... Robin Oakley pays tribute to the late David 'The Duke' Nicholson. *The Spectator, 9 October 2006*

BONES
'We keep getting reports about horses' bones being found, but to date we still haven't found Shergar' ... Police spokesman in Ireland, Chief Inspector Sean Feehily, confirming that the case is not yet closed. *Daily Express, 4 June 2006*

BOOED
'Cavalry Charge was sent off the odds-on favourite but was beaten by a short head. David was booed into the unsaddling enclosure – Frenchie and I hid in the weighing room!' ... Lord Vestey reminiscing following the death of David Nicholson on how he had ridden a loser for him at Plumpton once, with unexpected consequences. *Pacemaker, October 2006*

BOOK
'I wrote a book once and I pretty much pulled myself to pieces. I like doing that' ... Henry Cecil. *The Independent, 29 September 2005*

BOOKIE
'All the punters wanted their money – and I knew what Custer felt like' ... course bookie Raymond Winterton recalls the day Desert Orchid, the people's champion, won the Cheltenham Gold Cup. *Independent on Sunday, 13 March 2005*

'I wanted to be sure I was getting a heart that had been very little used' … Robin Oakley's punchline to a joke in which a transplant patient chose a bookmaker over an Olympic athlete when offered a donor for his operation. *The Spectator, 29 October 2005*

'I'm the kind of bloke who thinks big bookmakers should be hunted with dogs just for fun' … Peter Thomas. *Racing Post, 30 January 2006*

BOOZE

'The plan now is to have lots to drink' … Moscow Flyer trainer Jessica Harrington asked about future plans for the horse following the win over Azertyuiop at Sandown in December 2004.

'I was drinking myself to death. I just couldn't control it, couldn't stop' … candid confession from leading flat jockey Robert Winston on his battle with the bottle. *Racing Post, 4 December 2005*

'Leaving at 2am somewhat worse for wear, a disorientated Seeley joined the queue for taxis. Unable to remember his destination, Seeley told the driver to tour the hotels in the area until he saw the one where he was staying. Some 50 yards down the drive, he peered out of the rear of the car window and realised his error. He was charged 2euros for his pains' … 'Tattenham Corner' in *The Observer* recounts the tale of bookmaker Stan James' PR man, Nigel Seeley, who apparently over-indulged on hospitality for hacks ferried over to a plush Naas hotel to plug the firm's sponsorship of the King George Chase, before setting out to look for his hotel. *The Observer, 12 December 2004*

'Food's the only problem. But you can find good restaurants if you look, and anyway we generally do more drinking than eating' ... French trainer Guillaume Macaire enjoys his trips to Britain. *Racing Review, March 2002*

'Many poured booze into sealed plastic freezer bags and then taped them to their shins or back' ... Andy Lines, on how racegoers at the 2006 Kentucky Derby got round the ban on bringing in their own refreshments. *The Sportsman, 8 May 2006*

BORN
'Good trainers, like good wives, are born, not made' ... Stockbridge trainer H S Persse, in 1940. Having upset the women, he added: 'Without natural flair it is better to keep away from racing stables and to run a garage, for no amount of teaching will transform a horseman into a trainer of horses.'

BOTHERED
'I can't believe people running horses for £250,000 haven't even bothered to do a good job walking the course' ... John Francome, who did just that with jockey Ryan Moore, wondered why Notnowcato's pilot was the only rider who deserted the far side of the track to find faster going, which helped him win the Coral Eclipse,

beating Authorised, partnered by Frankie Dettori. *Channel 4 Racing, 7 July 2007*

BOXING CLEVER
'**Newcastle were playing Liverpool the other day but I went to Kelso to watch Mephisto. If you'd said to me two years ago that I'd give up my box at the football ground for a box at the racecourse I'd have said it wouldn't happen**' ... Newcastle fan turned racing nut, owner Graham Wylie. *Guardian, 12 March 2005*

BOY OR GIRL?
'**I have ridden against her and there was no way to tell whether she was a boy or girl. She is different from any woman I've seen in the past**' ... Frankie Dettori, being very complimentary to 24-year-old, British-born Canadian riding sensation, Jayne Wilson. *The Times, 11 August 2006*

BRAG
'**Betting in racing now is like playing brag against someone who's got £20bn when you've got a tenner**' ... former jockey Scobie Coogan, conveniently overlooking that there has never actually been a time when that was not the case. August 2006

BRAWL ASCOT
'**Brawl Ascot: More drunk punters arrested than England World Cup fans**' ... front page headline of *The Sun* on 23 June 2006, contrasting behaviour at Royal Ascot, where, it was claimed, 25

racegoers had been arrested in three days, and at the World Cup where, claimed the paper, England fans 'have been hailed the best in the world' for their peaceful conduct with only 13 arrested in three days.

BREAK
'Horses will break your bones, your bank and your heart' ... Simon Barnes, himself a sufferer from all three, on the inevitable price of owning a horse. *The Times, 4 November 2005*

BREAKDOWN
'Two months after leaving Godolphin, I was on the point of a nervous breakdown. I'd put my heart and soul into something and I felt my world had collapsed around me' ... trainer Jeremy Noseda on a traumatic parting of the ways in the mid-1990s.

BREAST FRIENDS
'One character proffers a piece of cardboard with holes cut out; further investigation reveals it as a "breastometer", designed to measure various sizes. Inexplicably, two females standing on cooling boxes appear keen to oblige him' ... one of the traditional sights at Pimlico on Preakness Stakes day, according to Nicholas Godfrey. *Racing Post, 23 May 2005*

BREECHES
'We almost thought of bringing Terry Biddlecombe out of retirement, but we couldn't find a pair of breeches big enough to

fit him!' ... owner Jim Lewis on finding a jockey for his November 2005 winner, Impek.

'He once rode for my uncle, and the horse dumped him going to the start. Lester sent my uncle the cleaning bill for his breeches' ... trainer David Barker after his Sierra Vista won a race named in Piggott's honour at Haydock in September 2006.

BREEDING

'The art of breeding is a fanciful and subjective art that does not need to be governed by the test tube and science' ... Jim Manton of Hereford writes to the *Racing Post* (29 April 2005) to express his opposition to the possible future cloning of racehorses.

'Psychology is a very important part of racing. You want beautiful looking people with courage. I try to buy brave horses' ... bloodstock agent Richard Galpin. *Racing Post, 17 May 2005*

'My research appears to suggest that in recent years racehorses have become so speedily bred that none of them truly stay much beyond a mile' ... systems analyst, Nick Mordin. *Racing Post Weekender, 12 June 2005*

'Several generations of the thoroughbred have been tested less rigorously than their antecedents, weaknesses have been left unexposed and as a consequence, we have a softer breed, more prone to unsoundness' ... Tony Morris questions the cult of watering. *Racing Post, 3 June 2005*

'Arab involvement, creating more jobs in racing and breeding, has generally been regarded as a good thing, but it has also, unquestionably, made it more difficult for the average person to buy quality bloodstock' … Lord Oaksey in his role as Club President of the Elite Racing Club in 2004.

'Breeding racehorses for a living is not something a sane, intelligent, mature person experienced in American capitalism would ever attempt to do' … but former *Chicago Tribune* editor Jim Squires gave up his job to do just that – and the grey colt he bred, Monarchos, went on to win the 2001 Kentucky Derby.

'The number of horses has increased year on year and is still rising, and sooner or later, numbers must outstrip demand' … timely 2004 warning by Doncaster Sales' MD, Henry Beeby.

'We desperately need breeders and even the sales companies to realise that racehorses, where the adjectives tough, consistent, sound, genuine and courageous apply, are nearly always the ones who win over a mile and a half or further. These, surely, are the stallions we should be sending our best mares to' … Ian Balding speaks up for stayers. *Racing Review, December 2001*

'Flat racing is a sport based on Darwinian principles; only the best get to breed, only the best get to become ancestors' … Simon Barnes. *The Times, 4 November 2005*

'**I think every mare in Britain should have to have a rating of 70 before she's allowed to breed**' ... substitute 'woman' for mare and IQ for 'rating' and Robin Bastiman would be on controversial ground. *Racing Post, 19 June 2006*

'**What a pity people don't take as much trouble with their own breeding as intelligent racehorse owners do**' ... the late and now permanently unwell journalist and racing buff, Jeffrey Bernard.

'**I always suspect that the improvement of the breed of horses means to get the best horse and to win the most money**' ... cynicism about breeding ruled even in the thoughts of early turf dictator, Admiral Rous (1795-1877), quoted by his biographer, T H Bird in 1939's *Admiral Rous and the English Turf*.

'**If the minimum distance of Flat races were two miles, the thoroughbred would be a much sounder breed. In breeding mainly for stamina, we would have indirectly infused durability and resilience into the racehorse**' ... James Willoughby. *Racing Post, 22 June 2006*

BRUTE FORCE
'**If you can convince them to give you everything from deep in their heart, as opposed to physically picking them up and throwing them back down again, you have something more powerful than brute force**' ... Canadian jockey Jayne Wilson on why strength is not the only ingredient in successful riding. She adds, 'I'm not a female

jockey, I'm a jockey that happens to be female.' *The Times, 11 August 2006*

BUBBLY
'I prepared for the race by putting a bottle of champagne in the fridge. Now I'm going to drink it' ... Olivier Peslier, having ridden Westerner to win the 2005 Ascot Gold Cup.

BUFFOON
'This buffoon has cost the industry £7m. The real winner was virtually unbacked but the horse we have to pay out on was a hot favourite. Her eyesight can't be trusted' ... bookie Barry Dennis is not best pleased as serial offender, judge Jane Stickels once again gave a corrected race result, at Lingfield on Monday, 6 March 2006. She first called 9/4 favourite Welsh Dragon the winner but later corrected herself in favour of 14/1 shot Miss Dagger – after the weigh-in.

BUILT UP AREA
'Folkestone next Friday is builders' day. There is a prize for the racegoer who looks most like they have just walked off a building site' ... Claude Duval reveals an innovative marketing ploy on 18 June 2005.

BULLY FOR HIM
'Taken by Prescott, they reveal in sequence on two walls of the conservatory, the final moment's of a bullfighter's life' ... Simon

Milham, who spent a day with bullfighting aficionado and top trainer Sir Mark Prescott, reveals the somewhat stark photographs on display in his home. *Pacemaker, July 2005*

BULLSH*T
'There's an awful lot of bullsh*t talked about training horses. It's just twice up the gallops every day and run them when you want' ... Philip Hobbs.

BUMS
'Don't ask me why, but going racing is what low-life bums do in New York' ... Charlie Brooks. *Daily Telegraph*, 10 October 2005

BUNGALOW WILL
'It's like attaching a factory chimney to a bungalow' ... Giles Coren on Willie Carson's Royal Ascot (at York) top hat. *The Times, 16 June 2005*

BURIED
'I want to be buried alongside Red Rum by the winning post' ... Aintree King, Ginger McCain, who describes himself as 'a broken down old taxi driver who has trained four winners of the National.' *The Sun, 8 April 2006*

'When I die, I'd like to be buried at Chester, if there's room' ... he wasn't, so perhaps it was full – journalist and racing fan, Jeffrey Bernard.

BUSINESS BUT NOT BUDDIES
'We lasted so long because it was business from both sides – we weren't buddies' ... George Duffield on announcing his retirement, commenting on his 30 year relationship with trainer Sir Mark Prescott. *Racing Post, 12 March 2005*

'You can learn more in a William Hill shop than at business school' ... Will Buckley. *The Observer, 24 April 2005*

BUZZ
'What struck me most was how you could have a great day at the races without ever seeing a horse. Every half-hour there's a great buzz of excitement as the race finishes, but there's so much other drama going on' ... Amanda Whittington, author of comedy drama play, *Ladies Day*, launched at the Hull Truck Theatre in June 2005.

CAR
'You can get to know your car a lot better than your girlfriend' ... former all weather champion jockey Jean-Pierre Guillambert on the sacrifices of racing at both day and night meetings during the summer. *The Sportsman, 21 September 2006*

CARNIVAL
'To me, it's a kind of carnival. The jockeys look like little harlequins when they come out into the paddock in their silks. And I've always thought horses were beautiful' ... top British artist and horse racing fan, Mark Wallinger. *FT How To Spend It Magazine, November 2005*

CASH

'There was all this crap in the papers about furthering his career. That's bollocks. He went to further his bank balance' ... owner Howard Johnson, who has most of his horses with Martin Pipe, is in no doubt why A P McCoy left there to join Jonjo O'Neill. *Pacemaker, March 2005*

'For every pound I put in, I do not expect to get back a penny. I haven't done it as an investment. If I want to invest money, it goes into a business and property portfolio' ... millionaire owner Graham Wylie is in no doubt about the financial implications of his hobby. *Daily Telegraph, 25 February 2005*

CEILING

'My head kept hitting the ceiling because they were giving me the bumps' ... Martin Pipe recalls celebrations with his staff in their local pub, after he clinched the trainer's title in 2004.

CELEBRATION

'His trademark celebration – tucking into a pile of local oysters he has brought with him from La Palmyre' ... Ben Newton reveals French trainer Arnaud Chaille-Chaille's favourite victory treat. *Racing Post, 4 March 2005*

'I drink plenty and I'm not saying I haven't celebrated my winners with the Channons and the Hannons, but are THEY too pissed to train their horses? I don't think so' ... David Elsworth tells Peter

Thomas that his reputation for enjoying a celebration does not mean he is not also a top trainer, who 'never missed a day's work in my life and I can still go to bed at three in the morning and be up again at six, first in the yard and ready to go.' *Racing Post, 13 June 2005*

'We celebrated okay, but it was a quiet party. We don't do wild' ... trainer Frances Cowley who became the first woman (officially) to train a Classic winner in Ireland when Saoire, ridden by Mick Kinane, won the 2005 Irish 1000 Guineas, on how she and husband jockey Pat Smullen, commemorated the occasion.

'Celebrate? The only way I can celebrate anything these days is by waking up alive' ... 83-year-old blind and infirm Australian Second World War veteran Allan Inglis, after backing Randwick winner Racing To Win to the tune of A$106,000 Aussie dollars – about £40,000 – in April 2006. He collected A$509,000

CELEBS
'A woman in our group backed a horse called Half Free because she had an on-off relationship, so she considered herself 'half-free'. It romped in at 33/1 and since then I've always looked at the names of horses for clues' ... soccer veteran, Sir Bobby Robson explains his winner-finding technique. *Mail on Sunday, 13 March 2005*

CERTAINTY
'The only certainty in thoroughbred horse breeding is the

uncertainty' … Lt-Col Giles Loder, trainer of 1920 Derby winner, Spion Kop.

CHAIRMAN
'He is the only person I know in our world who would be the chairman of a multi-national company in another life. The rest of us would be taxi drivers' … John Hammond is a fan of top French trainer Andre Fabre. *Daily Mail, 28 September 2006*

CHALK AND CHEESE
'You choose between robust, high class prose, and something akin to poetry' … Robin Oakley tries to sum up the contrast between A.P. McCoy and Timmy Murphy's styles. *The Spectator, 4 December 2004*

CHAMPAGNE
'Can I have yours, Saleem, you don't drink, do you?' … having shared the 2005 champion apprentice crown with Saleem Golam, the first female winner of the title, Hayley Turner, cheekily doubled her haul of champagne by commandeering her rival's.

'Get the f***in' bubbly open!' … an ecstatic Frankie Dettori bursts into the jockeys' changing room after winning the 2007 Derby – forgetting that he is being trailed by BBC TV cameras.

CHAMPION
'The season begins on January 1 and runs to December 31 and

the champion jockey – as with the champion trainer and champion owner – should be decided over the calendar year' ... I have to agree with *Racehorses of 2004*, discussing the Flat jockey title – but why shouldn't that reasoning also apply to the jump boys?

'We didn't have more than eleven winners for any one trainer.' ... agent Chris McGrath on Jamie Spencer's 2005 Flat-title winning season. *Daily Express, 1 December 2005*

CHARACTER
'She is a six furlong horse with a five furlong brain' ... Lydia Pearce on her sprinter Stargem in March 2005.

CHARIOT RACING
'When they had chariot racing, the guy drawn widest was in the same boat as trainers today. You just have to get on with it' ... trainer Gerard Butler on the draw at Chester. *Racing Post, 9 September 2006*

CHARISMA
'Charisma has bypassed the current crop of Flat jockeys' ... charismatic Charlie Brooks. *Daily Telegraph, 29 August 2005*

'Cigar made me want to be around horses, to truly fall in love with them. He was truly charismatic' ... his jockey, Jerry Bailey, on the 1996 Dubai World Cup winner.

CHAVS

'We have far too many chavs I'm afraid. I won't be asking visitors to wear morning coats but I would like to see the ladies in nice traditional English summer frocks, with linen suits and Panama hats for the gentlemen' … Goodwood's owner, the Earl of March, talking to the *Daily Mail*'s Richard Kay just before the 2007 Glorious Goodwood meeting.

CHEATING

'He was cheating the connections of the horses he rode in the eight races and the punters who bet on them' … Jockey Club disciplinary committee verdict on jockey Gary Carter, who they warned off for five years and fined £2,000 in October 2005.

'Will racing's practitioners ever be discouraged from cheating or is it just too ingrained in the psyche of the sport?' … Richard Griffiths. *The Sportsman, 18 June 2006*

'Football results are more at the mercy of the successful cheat than any horserace' … try as I might I cannot agree with Paul Haigh's assertion. *Racing Post, 8 July 2006*

'In the case of racing, there has been a reluctance to acknowledge that cheating is a regular occurrence at racecourses up and down the land. A wonderful array of terms has been used to camouflage the wrong doing, ranging from trainers being described as 'shrewd'

to the 'sympathetic' rides given by jockeys' ... editorial. *The Sportsman, 8 August 2006*

CHEMICAL

'Only in racing do guys become superstars at the snap of a finger. It ain't talent, baby, it's chemicals and painkillers, and we all know who the bums are' ... Richard Bomze, president of the New York Horseman's Association, on the threat to US racing of drugs cheats. *Racing Post, 29 May 2005*

'We're breeding a chemical horse. Nobody really knows the long-term effect of what those drugs will do. It's weakening the breed and it's dangerous' ... Arthur Hancock, breeder of Kentucky Derby winners Gato del Sol and Fusaichi Pegasus, and owner of Derby winner Sunday Silence, is apprehensive about some of the things administered to horses today. *Associated Press, 22 May 2006*

CHEQUE IT OUT

'I fractured my right wrist – so I won't be able to sign any cheques for a while' ... jockey Michael Kinane sees the positive side to an August 2005 injury.

CHILDREN

'Should children under 12, say, be allowed to attend the biggest race days? They make minimal contributions to the Tote pool and have maximum annoyance value when carried on the shoulders of

show-off men. Frankly, they are a nuisance' … no kidding! Laura Thompson. *Racing Post, 8 August 2006*

CHINESE WHISPERS
'Where else can I find a job where I do not see a bill, get a bloody good salary, have a driver, two interpreters and four people to each horse?' … now, let me see, er, no, Worcestershire trainer Nigel Smith is right. The four-horse handler applied on spec for a vacancy with the Beijing Jockey Club and came up trumps, beating 55 rivals, and starting his new post in China in January 2005.

CHIP
'I have only met about half a dozen trainers in my fifty years on the Turf who did not carry a chip on their shoulders the size of a telegraph pole' … veteran racing journalist Quentin Gilbey, in 1973.

CHURCH
'I couldn't go to the races and not have a bet. That would be the same as going to church and not praying' … high rolling Aussie punter Perce Galea in 1976, who regularly staked six figure sums on his horses. He died, aged 67 in 1977.

CLASSIC
'To me, English Classics are the great races in the world. It's the home of racing and any English Classic would be worth five French Classics' … Jeremy Noseda. *Racing Post, 3 September 2006*

CLASSIC BREEDING

'The proliferation of mile and a quarter events in the world calendar and the blind acceptance that a Classic winner must also win over the shorter distance to be regarded as a commercially attractive proposition can lead to only one thing – the further diminution of influence of the Classic thoroughbred' ... Greg Nicholls, BHB Chief Executive, at that organisation's 2005 annual review.

CLASSIC CHANGE

'There's no downside to putting the races back a fortnight and I'm sure it would give more of an opportunity for the most talented horses to win' ... Mick Channon floats his suggestion of putting back the Classics by two weeks. *Racing Post, 25 May 2005*

CLASSIC DOUBLE

'With Walter winning the Derby on Shergar, it robbed the Swinburns of a unique father and son Epsom Classic double and I thought it was utterly disgraceful' ... veteran racing writer George Ennor took over 20 years to forgive trainer Dermot Weld for 'jocking off Wally Swinburn from hot favourite Blue Wind in favour of Lester Piggott in the 1981 Oaks.' *2004 Horserace Writers & Photographers Annual Luncheon programme*

CLASSY

'He's a working-class horse; he does nothing but graft' ... trainer Steve Gollings detects blue-collar characteristics in his Haydock, December 2004 winner, Jack Martin.

CLERK OF THE COURSE
'The official kit for a clerk is a pointy stick and a Labrador – you have to provide the thick skin yourself' … Steve Dennis. *Racing Post, 11 August 2006*

CLOCK
'I check everything for the Arc weekend, from the menus to the going, but I didn't check the clock!' … chief executive officer of France Galop, Louis Romanet, admitting a five second difference between the reported and actual time of 2006 Arc winner, Rail Link.

CLONE VOICE
'It was a British discovery and we are not allowed to use it commercially – as ever, the rest of the world cashes in on our scientific discoveries' … Frankie Dettori's father in law, Professor Twink Allen, head of the Equine Fertility Unit at Newmarket, bemoans the fact that his efforts to clone horses, which could ultimately lead to the cloning of great racehorses, were thwarted, as news broke of the cloning of elite showhorses. *Daily Telegraph, 15 April 2005*

CLOTHES
'The trouble with some people is that they always want to buy horses in their best clothes – I've always said you should buy them in their working clothes and make them wear their best clothes later' … 73-year-old owner of top chaser Kingscliff, Arnie Sendell. *Pacemaker, January 2006*

'It is said that the only horse that most of them have anything to do with is a clothes horse' ... scornful comment about members of the French Jockey Club by Robert Black in his 1899 *Horse Racing In France*.

COAL COMFORT
'Dad had a coal mine which was doing well at the time, so after I rode the horses in the morning I'd have to go to work down the mine' ... Welsh jockey turned trainer John Llewellyn remembers his early, dual purpose days. *Racing Post Weekender, 8 December 2004*

COCKY
'Noel Meade said once in print that I was a cocky little bas*ard. I'd say it was probably true – I was always pretty sure of myself. If you don't believe in your own ability, then who will?' ... jockey Barry Geraghty. *Racing Post, 7 March 2005*

'Like all cocky teenagers I really thought I knew it all back then' ... Frankie Dettori on riding his first winner, Lizzy Hare, at Goodwood in 1987. *The Times, 26 July 2005*

'So cocky that if he was a sweet he would eat himself' ... Barry Dennis on Belgian superstar jock, Christophe Soumillon. *The Sun, 3 June 2006*

COFFIN

'We even stuck a form guide and racing paper in his coffin' ...
27-year-old Ross Plumber after his dad, publican Harry, 52, from
Darwen in Lancs, died and left instructions that instead of buying
flowers, mourners should back a horse called Time To Regret –
which duly won at 11/8 in January 2007. *Daily Mirror, 25
January 2007*

COINCIDENCE

**'If people think we view it as pure coincidence that runners drawn
high at Chester and low at Beverley are in good health before
declaration time, but then suddenly take a turn for the worse after
declaration time when the draw is revealed, they need to think
again'** ... Owen Byrne of the HRA, not happy after four horses – all
with vet certificates – declared non-runners at Chester happened to
have been drawn 14 of 14; 13 of 13; 12 of 12 and 9 of 9 in early
September 2006.

COLD

**'I don't think I've been on the cold trainers' list before, but I have
to say it's not that interesting a place to be in all honesty'** ...
Martin Pipe was relieved when his losing streak of 47 disappeared
thanks to Lough Derg at Exeter in mid-December 2005.

COLLAR BONE

'I think I've broken my left collar bone – it couldn't be the other

one as I've already had it removed' … Mick Fitzgerald recalls his reaction following a fall. *TalkSPORT, 20 October 2006*

COMEBACK
'When I stopped racing I lost my identity. I wasn't a rider any more, just a small bloke with black hair' … Derby-winning jockey Alan Munro on his comeback in March 2005.

'Its very disappointing, especially as I'm fitter and my arm is stronger now than in 1999' … former champion jump jockey Richard Dunwoody after his attempted comeback from retirement in 1999 was scuppered, in May 2005, by medical concerns that his neck was susceptible to fracture.

COMMENTATOR
'Calling a race is very similar to going on stage. Standing in the wings waiting to go on, you tend to think, "What the hell am I doing this for?" But when you're on stage, and when you come off at the end, it's such a massive natural high, that it reminds you why you do it' … Actor-turned-racecourse commentator, Malcolm Tomlinson. *Racing Post, 2 December 2004*

'It started with the usual shout "They're off" from the crowd and nothing was heard after that except the confused murmurs of the onlookers until the horses got round the notorious Tattenham Corner, then the commentator took up with "Ah, yes, here they come, they're getting down to it now – he's drawing ahead – it is

sure to be Lex – no, it's Harpagon"' … don't ever complain about commentaries today after hearing former legendary race-caller Raymond Glendenning discussing the BBC radio commentary of the 1926 Derby – won by neither Lex nor Harpagon, but Coronach.

'We will give a prize to the commentator if he pronounces the race title correctly' … Bangor clerk of the course Ed Gretton wasn't being as generous as it sounded when he offered Malcolm Tomlinson an incentive for 2005 race the 'Llanfairpwllgwyngyllgogerychwyrndrob-wllllantysiliogogogoch Handicap Hurdle.'

COMMITMENT
'The great strength of going racing at Cheltenham is that you know everyone around you has earned their right to be there by spending the winter standing in the open in rain, sleet, and freezing wind to follow their sport. That is the kind of commitment you only get from a true believer' … the late racing fan-cum-politician, Robin Cook.

COMPENSATION
'An increased chance of solvency has always seemed inadequate compensation for all the deprivations suffered by the substantial company of sports enthusiasts who have never seen the point about horse racing' … Hugh McIlvanney sympathises with those who don't like a flutter. *Sunday Times, 1 October 2006*

COMPLEXITY

'Maybe it's time for Channel 4, and the BBC for that matter, to try selling racing by braining it up rather than dumbing it down: to try selling it, in other words, without apology for its fascinating complexity but by making that complexity its selling point' ... Paul Haigh, whose own complexity is legendary. *Racing Post, 25 June 2005*

COMPROMISE

'One day I rode on the flat at Southwell, over hurdles at Towcester and then drove on to Windsor for an evening meeting. Safety has to be the first priority but jockeys must earn a living. There must be a compromise rather than a ban' ... jockey Vince Slattery, showing that he just didn't get it as he argued against a proposed ban on jockeys riding at more than one meeting per day, hot on the heels of jockey Neil Callan's 12 month driving ban for speeding at 107mph as he raced to get to Goodwood in time. *News of the World, 6 August 2006*

CONCEAL

'I would say the racing authorities do their very best to conceal these routine deaths. They are as predictable as they are depressing because of the demands the industry places on these increasingly overworked animals' ... yes, Animal Aid spokesman Andrew Tyler, would say that – and did after nine horses died at the Cheltenham Festival in 2006.

CONCRETE

'If you lose, you're concrete. If you win, you can have Belinda for the night' ... syndicate manager Henry Ponsonby recalling a colourful member from the East End, who once arrived at the races with his glamorous blonde companion on his arm as he issued riding instructions to an un-named jockey. *News Weekend, 3 September 2005*

CONDEMN

'Instead of trying to condemn the man we should celebrate him, not like a lot of geniuses are, after they are dead and gone for twenty years' ... Aidan O'Brien supports Kieren Fallon. *Racing Post, 15 July 2006*

CONFESSION

'I'm totally unfit, to be honest, and got unbalanced in the closing stages. I'm an office man and only ride about once a fortnight. Even when I gave my mount a slap I actually missed' ... racegoers were sceptical about 28-year-old amateur rider Michael Purcell's excuses after he was banned for 50 days after being beaten a length for a 'motionless' ride on Laetitia at Cork – by well backed (7/1 from 14/1) stable companion Alpha Royale.

CONSPIRACY

'Shamefully, the momentum behind this conspiracy of silence has been maintained by the racing media' ... James Willoughby criticises colleagues for not investigating adequately the controversial state of the ground at York's June 2005 'Royal Ascot' meeting.

CONTAMINATION

'It is difficult to think of a sport that has not in some way been contaminated by the pressures of modern life – apart, that is, from National Hunt racing' … Terence Blacker. *The Independent, 18 March 2005*

CONTRACT

'This is my eleventh year in the job and I have never had a contract in all that time. It is all done on a handshake.'…Frankie Dettori on his boss Sheikh Mohammed *News Times, 26 March 2005*

COP THAT

'The main crime is pickpocketing, so racegoers beware' … .Chief Inspector Ian Jones with a warning to 2005 Cheltenham Festival attendees.

CORE

'How long will racing's core audience – the traditional middle-class racegoer – put up with the noise, discomfort and offensive behaviour of racegoers, some of whom are the worse for drink before they pass through the turnstiles?' … Julian 'Mr Angry' Wilson does not like the upsurge of boozy behaviour at the races.

COUNSELLORS

'There should be two or three counsellors spread around the country with the job of helping jockeys. Three years ago I'd have

picked up the phone to someone like that, but I hope they might
have spotted that I was in trouble, too, and come to me first' ...
Robert Winston calling for more help for jockeys suffering from all
manner of problems. *The Times, 6 March 2007*

COUNTED DOWN
'He loved his racing and I am so glad we managed to have a
winner for him with old Mare of Wetwang' ... trainer James Bethell
playing tribute to presenter of Channel 4's Countdown, Richard
Whiteley, keen racegoer, owner and one time Mayor of the village of
Wetwang – hence the name of his winner – who died aged 61 in
June 2005.

COUNTENANCE
'There is certainly no sense of wealth or joie de vivre from the dark
countenance he brings to the racecourse' ... Richard Edmondson
on racing tycoon John Magnier. *The Independent, 4 October 2005*

COURAGE
'What women jockeys need is someone with the courage to break
the mould and put a woman up on a really good horse'...promising
jockey Hayley Turner, spotlighting one of the reasons that she and
her fellow lady riders find it so difficult to break through.' She adds,
in a slightly unfortunate phrase: 'I think a lot more trainers are
coming around but it's the owners that we have to sell ourselves to
now.' *Guardian, 14 September 2005*

COURSE I DON'T LIKE IT

'It may be the home of racing, but for punters and spectators on TV and at the track, the place is a total shambles.' … racing writer Tom Segal on Newmarket's Rowley Mile course.

'A dump' … commentator and journalist Iain Mackenzie voices his opinion of Tipperary on At The Races in August, 2005.

COURSING

'It's a magnificent track for its size and sets standards for all small tracks in Britain' … trainer Mark Johnston is a fan of Hamilton racecourse. *Daily Telegraph, 14 June 2005*

COWBOYS

'The 10 strong party of City boys who came wearing OK Corral style cowboy hats and Mexican sombreros may have been oblivious to racing tradition' … mmm, not much gets past Jamie Reid, does it? He was right, though – I also saw the lads who were at Sandown for the Tingle Creek Chase clash between Moscow Flyer and Azertyuiop in December 2004, and form comparison was not their main concern of the day. *Guardian, 6 December 2004*

CRAZY

'It's the craziest betting race I've ever seen in my life' … Mike Dillon of Ladbrokes on the sheer volume of support for Deep Impact – much of it from up to 5,000 Japanese racegoers – to win the 2006 Arc, which forced the Japanese raider as short as 1/10 at one point, starting at 1/2 on the Pari Mutuel when odds of up to 5/2 were available with traditional bookmakers. Winner, Rail Link, went off at 24/1 instead of a predicted 8/1 as a result.

CREAM
'I don't even like cream' … newly crowned 2005 Champion Jockey, Jamie Spencer, who was just about to receive his trophy at Doncaster on 5 November, when fellow rider Tony Culhane splattered him in the face with a cream cake.

CRICKETERS
'We were told about drugged cyclists, weary cricketers, Formula One and far too much about the start of the football season, but not a single word on one of the most exciting Group 1 horse races in living memory' … broadcaster Robert Cooper is not impressed that the BBC 10pm News sports round-up did not regard the Ouija Board versus Alexander Goldrun battle at Glorious Goodwood worthy of mention. *The Sportsman, 8 August 2006*

CRIME
'We should be grateful, I suppose, that he did not grab the beast by the ears, drag its head down and kick its teeth in. Even had he done this it would have been a crime scarcely comparable with the 5,000 'retired' horses sent to the abbatoir each year, the thousands of colts put down because they didn't quite make the grade, the hundreds of horses killed or maimed going over fences' … *Sunday Times'* columnist Rod Liddle shows that racing is not

universally revered, in a piece about head-butting jockey Paul O'Neill's one-day punishment. *6 August 2006*

CRISIS?
'Racing always appears to be in one crisis or another ... **maybe most of these crises are more about perception than reality'** ... BHB Chairman, Martin Broughton. *The Times, 14 December 2004*

CROSSWORDS
'They are the cryptic crosswords of racing once you get one line of reasoning right, other clues fall into place' ... Lydia Hislop on handicaps. *The Times, 13 September 2006*

CRUEL
'People paint this sport as cruel, but when a horse dies, no one hurts more than race people' ... Tony McCoy. *Daily Telegraph, 25 March 2006*

CRYING
'I didn't cry when I scored a try for Wales schoolboys against France at Cardiff Arms Park and I didn't cry when I scored the winning try for Gloucester in a John Player Cup semi-final, but I bawled my eyes out when Davoski won and unashamedly so' ... trainer/ jockey cum GP and former rugby star, Dr Philip Pritchard on the delights of training a 50/1 Cheltenham winner secured on 14 November 2004.

'It is one of the few times on television I actually felt like crying. It is one of the saddest things I have ever had to deal with in racing' … what devastating tragedy can have afflicted Tony McCoy in May 2006? No deaths, no destruction – he was reacting to news of Martin Pipe's retirement.

CULTURE
'The racing culture you have is second to none. It's the only place I know where racing is part of the national fabric and not a niche sport.' … .Luca Cumani on why he intends to stay in England rather than return to his native Italy. *Racing Post, 13 August 2006*

CYNICAL – OR SICK?
'As the screens went up, so did the horse's Kempton price, with £18 matched at 46 and another tenner at 38' … Graham Wheldon highlights Exchange trading and the cynicism of punters, which saw Our Vic's odds for the forthcoming King George Chase lengthening even as the horse lay on the ground, possibly dying, after taking a fall at Cheltenham on 11 December 2004. He recovered. *Racing Post, 13 December 2004*

'Inevitably there will be some people who will try to benefit from the death of a horse' … commented Betfair's Tony Calvin in December 2005 as the Exchange endeavoured to prevent them from doing so, by voiding such bets, having apparently only just noticed what was going on. *Guardian, 16 December 2005*

DADDY LONGLEGS
'The leatherjackets explanation certainly looks the most plausible cause' ... Chepstow clerk of the course, Tim Long, explaining that a variety of daddy-longlegs was being blamed for causing problems with the track's racing surface which resulted in two nasty incidents of jockey injury, and a horse having to be destroyed. The insects lay eggs in the grass and emerging bugs then feed on roots, weakening the strength of the grass's grip on the soil.*Racing Post, 6 September 2005*

DATE
'My dad knew he didn't have much time left and suggested I ring up Ladbrokes and try to get a price that he went out on the same date he came in' ... John Christie, who didn't take the tip before his bookie father Roy died on his 80th birthday in June 2006. I'd have offered 80/1!

DEADBEATS
'Racing is the sport of kings and deadbeats' ... interesting variation on the old cliché by Jim Haynes, an entertainer who put together a 2005 CD, *Great Australian Racing Stories*.

DEAD CERT
'It's sickening that racehorse owners must not only suffer the distress of losing their horses but must also pay a forfeit they cannot avoid.' ... trainer Alan Bailey, who declared a dead horse for the 1996 Royal Hunt Cup, hoping it would miss the cut and thus enable its entry money of £360 to be refunded.

'He actually died for six minutes under the anaesthetic at the Horsham veterinary practice' … yet Raahin, owned by former jockey Ron Atkins, recovered and won a hurdle race at Fontwell in January 1995.

'Constantly, when you have horses you are going to have dead horses. It's a fact of life. I'm not hardened to it … the worst thing is the empty stable.' … Moscow Flyer's trainer Jessica Harrington. *Daily Telegraph, 12 November 2005*

'We're dead mate, this is it, we're gone' … fortunately premature comment by Frankie Dettori to fellow passenger and rider Ray Cochrane as their plane crashed in June 2001.

DEATH BED
'People say they would get off their death bed to ride the Gold Cup favourite. AP would get off his death bed to ride in a Taunton seller' … Richard Dunwoody on the equally committed Tony McCoy in March 2006.

DEATH IN THE AFTERNOON
'I didn't know Tom personally, but that doesn't matter, he was one of our own. He went out there with the rest of us, he was one of us' … jump jockey Graham Lee pays tribute to 20-year-old Tom Halliday, killed in a Market Rasen fall in July 2005.

'X-rays revealed that Horatio Nelson had suffered several fractures

of the cannon and sesamoid bones and dislocation of the fetlock joint. Sadly, the injuries were considered to be too severe to be repaired and the horse has therefore been euthanised' ... carefully structured announcement by Paul Struthers, PR manager for the Horseracing Regulatory Authority which could not, though, disguise the fact that the well fancied 2006 Derby runner from Aidan O'Brien's stable had been destroyed.

'Valiramix was an especially lovely horse and we kept his box empty for about six weeks. Whenever you walked past you felt his death all over again' ... unexpectedly raw emotion from Martin Pipe, in an interview with Donald McRae. *Guardian, 3 October 2006*

DEBATE
'There will always be debate about aspects of horseracing, not least how to spell the word or words – is it horseracing; horse-racing or horse racing?' ... you may well ask and neither I nor racing author Wray Vamplew can decide.

DEBAUCHERY
'If a person wishes to witness debauchery and a set of semi-intoxicated, soft brained noodles, misnamed men, I would counsel that person to frequent the course' ... hardly a ringing testimonial to South Africa's Durban racecourse, visited in 1880 by English racing fan, John William Coleman.

DECEIT
'Too widely are racing's known practices of deceit and profiteering met with a slap on the back or blind eye by those with an ethical obligation to expose them' ... Lydia Hislop. *The Times, 23 December 2005*

DECENT
'I can be a decent human at 8st 4lb, but I can't be a saint even at 9st 7lb' ... Lester Piggott in 1970.

DEDICATION
'For all fathers and sons separated by the generation gap' ... Bill O'Gorman in his 2005 book, *Racing Horses*.

DEER DAY OUT
'They delayed the start of the race while racetrack staff together with 150 spectators tried to get the animals back in the park' ... Eye witness Kirsten Bansdorf explains how 50 escaped deer caused the abandonment of a meeting at Copenhagen's Klampenborg racetrack on 31 August 1996.

DEFEAT
'Defeat is an important – perhaps the most important – part of the sporting life. Certainly, football fans and those who bet on horses know that' ... Simon Barnes. *The Times, 19 May 2006*

DERBY

'How anyone can say its better on a Saturday is just beyond belief and if the Epsom executive goes on about how many more people go these days just tell them to get the Sugababes to play on the Wednesday instead' ... 'hear, hear', say I to Tom Segal's opinion that Derby Day is Wednesday. *Weekender, 15 December 2004*

'Racing has shot itself in the foot by moving the race to Saturday. On Wednesday it was racing's big day but now it is just like any other Saurday fixture' ... Mick Channon, *Daily Express, 28 May 2006*

'It's little things that make English racing special, like the Derby being run on the worst track in the world' ... Mick Channon, echoing Julian Wilson's 1988 comment, 'it has always been a mystery to me why our best race should be run on our worst racecourse.' Channon later added, 'It should take place on the best racecourse which has to be Ascot.' *Daily Telegraph, 14 April 2006.*

'People talk about Derby experience, but I can't have it myself. It's just another race over a mile and a half on good horses. If anything it's easier' ... Ian Mongan is unimpressed with the mystique of the Derby prior to his debut ride in 2006 on Before You Go. *Racing Post, 28 May 2006*

'Neither the richest race in the world, nor the oldest thoroughbred classic, and run on a course that offers little more than rudimentary facilities to patrons, the English Derby is the greatest

of horse races' ... Aussie racing writer, Peter Pierce, 1994
'Betwixt York and Hull, deep in the heart of the East Riding of Yorkshire, the Kiplingcotes Derby has been staged every year since 1519. Remarkably the race has had a winner every year' ... that's what you call tradition! *Paul Davies, Racing Ahead, March 2005*

'I just love the Derby. It's a bit rough but then so are most of the people who go to it. The fun is that it's all a bit flash, brassy and dodgy' *Daily Telegraph, 6 June 2005*

'I've lived all of my life with the hope of winning the Derby – I know I'm almost certainly not going to now, but I can still dream' ... actor Omar Sharif in July 2005 when he was 73.

'It is too hard a race for three-year-olds. It has not produced a decent stallion in years and lives on its reputation' ... French trainer Andre Fabre reported by Richard Edmondson. *The Sportsman, 31 May 2005*

'I was tense before the race, though I was expecting him to win. I have found, if you think you've got a chance of winning the Derby, then you'll be tense beforehand. The fact that you have won the race before does not come into it. You still get tense' ... Michael Stoute thinks back to Shergar's Derby triumph in 1981. *Daily Telegraph, 1 June 2006*

'The 2006 Vodafone Derby has 18 runners – the biggest field for the premier Classic in the last ten years apart from the 20 who

lined up in 2003' ... so – not the biggest field for ten years at all, then – just the biggest for three years! Official Epsom racecourse press release.

'Dr Who and all the Daleks wouldn't stop me' ... jockey Martin Dwyer, who suffered a tumble at Bath the evening before he was due to partner Sir Percy in the 2006 Derby, causing doubts about his participation – the combination then got up on the line to win.
'Just another trial, albeit a magnificent and historic one, for the great clashes later in the season' ... Paul Haigh on the Derby.
Racing Post, 3 June 2006

'A few days before the Derby was to be run, I was at a private party at which there was a fortune teller. I was persuaded to have my fortune told. "You are going to win a big race; I think it is the Derby," the fortune-teller said. "You're telling me!" I replied' ... she was right – the Maharajah of Rajpipla was indeed owner of the 15/2 winner of the 1934 Derby, Windsor Lad. He would also win the Irish and Indian versions.

'I got stopped for speeding coming here, and though I told the policeman that I had the third favourite in the Derby, he was not impressed' ... but it was Marcus Tregoning's lucky day – the cop let him off and Sir Percy won the 2006 Derby.

'You've got some of the best-bred beasts on the planet mixing it with some rum old nags – and that's just in the Grandstand' ...

racing writer Simon Godley on 2006 Derby day. He also noticed a contemporary feature of the event: 'Up on the grandstand roof, police snipers lay poised to take out any terrorist suspects'. *The Sportsman, 4 June 2006*

'I was in a helicopter and leaving Epsom within thirty minutes of the weigh-in. It left me with an empty feeling' ... Mick Kinane could have done with more time to celebrate his 1993 Derby victory on Commander In Chief.

'The great difference between Derby Day crowds then and now is easily explained. Sixty years ago they were holiday-makers almost to a man and woman; nowadays they are racing enthusiasts pure and simple' ... no, not said recently – but in 1921 by racing writer Alexander Scott, who had attended 54 consecutive Derby days.

'These days, even winning the Derby could be putting a dampener on a horse's stud career, which is why most of the time they try to enhance their stud value by getting them a win over a mile and a quarter too' ... trainer William Haggas. *Guardian, 4 September 2006*

DESCRIPTION
'Look at him. A proper cripple, walks like a car park attendant' ... trainer Ian Semple's bizarre description of his sprinter, Chookie Heiton. *Guardian, 1 April 2005*

'He's a man who can't get out of bed in the morning without somebody putting his shoes out for him' … Clare Balding on Ginger McCain. *Guardian, 1 April 2005*

DETRIMENT
'They have sold racing to the detriment of genuine turf lovers, whose enjoyment of big race days is now compromised by moneyed chavs not remotely passionate about the sport of kings, but simply there to "have it large"' … *Racing Post* letter writer Rob Furber was unhappy at what he saw as the 'alcohol-fuelled atmosphere' of Newmarket on 2006 2000 Guineas day. *Racing Post, 10 May 2006*

DIE
'I actually thought I was going to die' … Kieren Fallon remembering a Royal Ascot 2000 fall on Alhawa. *The Sportsman, 9 July 2006*

'If I had known that night what Russian Hero was going to do today, I would have let him die' … Dick Francis wasn't being serious on the night he finished second on Roimond in the Grand National behind Russian Hero who, just a year earlier, he had helped save when he was struck down with potentially fatal colic. *The Sportsman, 27 August 2006*

DIED
'I've died and gone to heaven' … I am absolutely sure that no Ryanair passenger would ever have uttered a 'we should be so lucky'

after hearing Michael O'Leary, owner of both that airline and 2006 Cheltenham Gold Cup winner War Of Attrition trying to describe his feelings after victory in the race.

DIFFERENCE

'I think the difference between a million-dollar horse and a $250,000 horse is not four times as great. Sometimes it's just a minuscule difference in quality and a gigantic difference in money.' ... Cot Campbell of Dogwood Stables speaking sense at the 2006 Saratoga Select Yearling Sale.

'I suppose having a jockey on board makes a difference, although sometimes the trainer might as well issue the instructions to the horse' ... David Ashforth. *Racing Post, 11 May 2006*

DIFFICULT

'Am I That Difficult? Handicap Hurdle' was the title given to a race he sponsored at Taunton in January 1997 by Martin Pipe.

DISGRACE

'Ferris's conduct was a complete disgrace. It showed a persistent and wilful disregard for the standard of honesty that the integrity of racing requires' ... HRA disciplinary panel report as Fran Ferris received a five year ban for allegedly riding horses to lose. *Racing Post, 22 April 2007*

DISGRACEFUL
'Who, for example, will sit around a table to discuss the rather less glamorous issue of why a cheese sandwich on the Rowley Mile costs a wholly disgraceful £4' ... Nick Luck asks the pertinent catering question. *The Sportsman, 8 May 2006*

DISH IT UP
'I was born to ride horses, not to do the dishes' ... Tony McCoy explains to the *Racing Post*'s Peter Thomas why he is happy to have his life organised by others. *Racing Post, 9 March 2005*

DISORIENTATED
'Racegoers at the Curragh might have become disorientated when the racecard cover for Saturday's 2000 Guineas depicted Attraction's 1000 Guineas victory the previous year. Symmetry was duly delivered when Sunday's racecard for the 1000 Guineas featured Bachelor Duke's 2000 Guineas victory 12 months earlier' ... Julian Muscat. *The Times, 26 May 2005*

DISREPUTE
'There has to be a point where if someone oversteps the boundaries of normal and fair criticism we will look into whether they are bringing the sport into disrepute' ... Jockey Club PR, Paul Struthers warning that the organisation was getting fed up with critics, particularly trainer Charlie Mann. *Racing Post, 4 February 2006*

DITCH
'I once spent the night with a girl in the ditch of the celebrated Pond Fence at Sandown ... perhaps I was pointing out to her that obstacle's peculiar hazards' ... the late, lamented and often 'unwell' racing raconteur, Jeffrey Bernard in 1987.

DIVINE
'There's no divine right to stay at the top level. It's the same in racing as football – if you haven't produced you take the consequences' ... Mike Channon, contemplating the relegation from the Premiership in May 2005 of two of the clubs he played for before becoming a trainer – Norwich and Southampton. *The Times, 20 May 2005*

DOGGING
'From what I hear, the Ascot Authority is still keeping quiet on the subject of which of their many car parks has been designated for dogging; they aren't really moving with the times' ... Sir Clement Freud on the new Ascot. *Racing Post, 31 May 2006*

DON'T BEAT ABOUT THE BUSH
'His Breeders' Cup rides on both Antonius Pius in the Mile and Powerscourt in the Turf made me want to open up the sick bag by my sofa and fill it with my recently digested Welsh rarebit!' ... columnist Paul Jacobs is no fan of Jamie Spencer. *Inside Edge, January 2005*

DOPEY?

'(Martin) Pipe gets a relatively small fine for refusing to cooperate in a drugs test, whilst (Rio) Ferdinand got a long ban for apparently forgetting to show up for his. Something doesn't seem right here.' ... Steve Mellish is baffled over an apparent anomaly as Martin Pipe rebels against drugs test because of concerns over hygiene. *Racing & Football Outlook, 1-7 March 2005*

'Who, me or the horse?' ... dreadlocked groom Glenroy Brown on being told that his Epsom winner Swan Maiden had been selected for a dope test on August 29, 2005.

'They won't let us dope the horses, so I'm doping myself' ... jump jockey Paddy Cowley, whilst knocking back a 'stiffish glass' of brandy before going out to ride, to racing historian John Fairfax-Blakeborough before a chase at Shincliffe, Co Durham just prior to the First World War. Sadly, Cowley was killed shortly afterwards, at Blackpool races.

DOSH

'I'm driven by dosh' ... unusually frank admission by a trainer – Eddie Hales after his 8/1 shot Public Reaction was a winner at Thurles in December 2005.

DREAM

'What gets me up at five every morning is that element of living in a dream factory' ... trainer Mick Channon. *The Times, 20 May 2005*

'For years I've dreamed about winning this race, ever since I was an apprentice with Kevin Prendergast – it means everything' … Kieren Fallon after winning the Irish Derby on Hurricane Run, in June 2005

'I had a dream that his bridle broke before the start and I had to borrow one of Aidan O'Brien's and then the horse won. It was quite bizarre that it actually happened' … Andrew Balding had to wake up and convince himself that his Phoenix Reach had indeed won the Hong Kong Vase on 12 December 2004

DRESSING UP
'Until an authority offers prize money to whoever wears the most comfortable boiler suit and finds a diminution in attendance as a consequence, I shall continue to resent dressing up to witness my favourite sport' … Sir Clement Freud. *Racing Post, 17 August 2005*

'I've learnt how to dress at race meetings now, but the first time I went to Royal Ascot I wore tails and a bow tie, which was a major mistake. People were openly laughing. I looked like a waiter' … actor/racehorse owner Nathaniel Parker, also a serious punter, who claims, 'I fund my racehorse hobby out of my winnings', adding 'out of 14 years of serious betting there have been only two years when I've made a loss'. *Mail on Sunday, July 2006*

DRINK
'I thought I'd got the job done as long as I didn't put the wrong

saddle on, which in the old days, I did when I'd had a drink' ...
Henry Cecil on preparing his two Oaks runners in 2007 – Light Shift
won.

DRUMS
**'I put the drum kit in the garage and then sold it to the blacksmith
years ago'** ... Richard Hannon, who drummed with an early version
of the hit-making group, The Troggs, many years ago. *Pacemaker,
June 2005*

DUCKY
**'I have six pairs of ducks. I've got a pair of black-necked swans as
well as some peacocks, golden and silver pheasants and loads of
hens'** ... duck-loving jockey Michael Hills. *Racing Post, 21 April
2005*

DUNG
'When you do dung it's nice to do it on your own muckheap' ... as
ever Ginger McCain finds the right phrase as he enjoys a May 2006
double at his local track, Bangor.

EARLY
'Like most men, he came too early' ... the *Racing Post* would not
reveal the identity of either the female trainer or the jockey on her
horse at York in July 2006. Spoilsports.

EARLY RETIREMENT
'All that is now expected of the few good two years old, who pass sufficiently uninjured through the ordeal of training, is to win two or three of the great two or three years old stakes; after which the owners are contented with their services in the stud' ... not a contemporary moan about early equine retirement, but the words of racing writer J C Whyte in 1840.

EARS
'Small ears may be all right on a Hollywood star but not on a racehorse' ... trainer H S Perrse – who trained the great The Tetrarch – in 1940, adding 'I have never yet trained a horse with short prick ears and a pig-eye that was not a rogue.'

EARTHQUAKE
'We are in the middle of an earthquake here in Southern California – Lady Lucayan tries to slow it down. She leads by two and a half lengths. By the way folks, I'd like you to know I love you all and that horse racing was my first love' ... US commentator Vic 'Goof on the Roof' Strauffer, commentating on a race at Hollywood Park in June 2005 during the course of which an earthquake began.

ECSTASY
'Races begin and end in an ecstasy of inexactness that adds a further frisson of excitement to the action' ... Steve Dennis on racing at Jersey's Les Landes course which has neither starting stalls nor photo finish equipment. *Racing Post, 3 September 2006*

EDUCATION

'If you want an education, education, education you should put in the hours at Sandown, Taunton and Fakenham' ... writer Will Buckley believes that life wisdom is better experienced on a racecourse than in the halls of academe. He supported his case by pointing out that 'Damon Runyan spent a lifetime at the track, zero time in the library and managed to write 80 million words.' *The Observer, 24 April 2005*

EFFECT

'I believe what makes the difference is the effect he has on all the others. He is the boss and if you take those who admire him and those who respect him he has an advantage' ... trainer Cedric Boutin on his one time apprentice, jockey Christophe Soumillon. *The Sportsman, 29 May 2006*

EMBARRASSMENT

'He's always telling me not to drop my hands, possibly because he has done that a few times and knows the embarrassment' ... fledgling jockey Patrick Hills on advice from dad, Richard. *Racing Post, 27 September 2006*

END OF THE WORLD

'It will do me good to see what really matters in life. We get so wrapped up in ourselves as jockeys. Often I've left somewhere after getting beat on two favourites and thought the world had come to an end' ... Jamie Spencer, prior to visiting Zambia on behalf of Barney Curley's Aid for Africa charity. *The Times, 25 July 2006*

ENTHUSIAST
'The racing enthusiast doesn't care about 0-70 handicappers running around the place, they care about watching good races' ... Jeremy Noseda. *The Sportsman, 8 May 2006*

EPITAPH
'Persian Punch – one of the finest horses to race on top of the Downs' ... stone plaque commemorating the people's favourite whose ashes were scattered at Goodwood. *The Observer, 1 May 2005*

ERROR
'I made a basic error and one which is forgivable when a boy but not as a leading rider. I picked my whip up in my hand after the last fence when I should have sat still to keep the tired chaser balanced' ... Richard Pitman is still beating himself up about Crisp just being beaten on the run in by future triple winner Red Rum in the 1973 Grand National. *Guardian, 1 December, 2005*

ETIQUETTE
'A cheery "how-do, missus?", followed by a bone-crushing handshake probably won't cut the mustard – more's the pity' ... tongue-in-cheek advice from the *York Evening Press* for readers on what to do if meeting the Queen at the 2005 rescheduled Royal Ascot at York meeting.

EUPHEMISTICALLY SPEAKING
'Pimlico needs to be re-located. It's in a no-walking-around zone,

if you know what I mean' ... *Racing Post* US correspondent on the charms of the course which stages the American Classic, the Preakness Stakes. *Racing Post, 27 May 2005*

EVERYBODY OUT
'It's just mob rule. These jockeys are getting like footballers. They are just too big for their boots' ... Anthony Cann, owner of intended runner Fine Times, was not best pleased when 21 jockeys – including Dettori, Eddery and Fallon, went on strike at Haydock in October 1996 after deciding the course was in a dangerous state because of heavy rain.

EXAM
'It is as if I am a school master. The owners are the parents, the horses the children, and the racecourse is the exam' ... scholarly explanation of his trade by Sir Mark Prescott.

EXCHANGES
'The betting exchanges are a big negative. I could go out on a favourite, ride an honourable race, run into trouble, get beat and then someone's had a lot of money on you to get beat. There's some possible link-up between me and that person and I'm innocent. That seems to be what's happening recently' ... jockey Alan Munro. *The Sunday Times, 27 March 2005*

'My instincts tell me that those who condoned the introduction of exchanges have created a dangerous cocktail that has already, and

will continue, to bring racing into disrepute' … former BHB Chairman, Peter Savill. *Racing Post, 13 April 2005*

'I am totally against them, I don't agree with them. It bangs the racing out to people who like skulduggery and it's just not the way forward for me.' *Richard Hannon, Pacemaker, June 2005*

'Subjective arguments from vested interests about them being either heaven-sent or the devil's work are an insult to our intelligence' … gamekeeper turned poacher, Sean Boyce, of At The Races, formerly of Ladbrokes, on the exchanges. *December 2004*

'Time will tell whether they are as good for punters as many believe. Just don't tell me they are good for racing' … *Guardian* racing writer, Ron Cox on betting exchanges. *Guardian, 13 October 2005*

'The British licensing of Betfair is clearly the worst mistake in the history of government racing administration. The second worst has been the refusal of the British administration to admit they have actually made an error' … not a great fan, then? Peter Fletcher, executive with Aussie betting organisation, Tabcorp, reported by Howard Wright. *Racing Post, 2 June 2006*

'We are supposed to believe that the exchanges have come to clean up. Personally, I wouldn't want to be the client of any outfit that boasts about its ability to place me in the dock.' *Tony Morris, Pacemaker, August 2006*

EXCREMENT

'The sight and sound of whizzing, whirling wheels on a jackpot machine may have the same appeal to some racecourse executives as catching the sole of a shoe in dog excrement, but sooner or later (virtual) reality racing is going to come into the sphere of real racing' ... Howard Wright, contemplating 'racinos'. *Racing Post, 27 January 2006*

EXCUSES, EXCUSES

'Some woman leaning over the rails started to 'click-click-click' like mad and it just set him alight. Rakti was on edge after that' ... jockey Philip Robinson on why the notoriously neurotic 5/6 favourite, Rakti, was spooked before his Royal Ascot (at York) defeat by Valixir in the 2005 Queen Anne Stakes.

'There are a few excuses that I could come up with but only one real one springs to mind. Ability. Lack of it.' ... Vince Slattery's judgement on St George's Girl, the 150/1 shot he had just pulled up at Leicester in December 2004.

'At Caulfield the grass was cut short, like in Japan. But, here at Flemington, the grass was too long' ... Japanese jockey Shinji Fujita comes up with an excuse to explain why his 2005 Melbourne Cup third favourite Eye Popper – on whom he had finished 2nd in the Caulfield Cup, could only manage 12th place, having run wide rather than on the rails as preferred by locals.

'**Unfortunately for him and for the blacksmith, he lost two shoes. It can't be that difficult to stick four shoes on a horse and it is always disappointing when 50 per cent of them fall off**' ... Henry Daly after his Downs Folly was a beaten favourite at Hereford in December 2005.

'**One or two trainers have called to say that seagulls and rooks drop stones on to their gallops at home, and I suppose it's plausible the same thing has happened to us**' ... Kempton clerk of the course Brian Clifford clutching at straws by suggesting birds clutching at stones may have been responsible for the large stones found on the track's new Polytrack surface before its debut meeting on Saturday, 25 March 2006.

'**Barry Hills informed us that the collision had been caused partly by his own horse running green (regulation excuse) and partly by the winner being startled by a pair of ambulance drivers (sly new one)**' ... Peter Thomas (*Racing Post*) on the coming together of third placed Alhaajes and winner Galient at Newmarket on 19 April 2006.

EXHIBIT
'**Remember, you are riding to exhibit the horse, not yourself**' ... advice from former great jump jockey-turned-trainer Stan Mellor, recalled by Peter Scudamore. *Daily Mail, 29 December 2005*

EXPENDABLE
'**The people who suffer when racing is shown to be corrupt are**

only the punters, and they – or we – have always been considered
expendable' ... Peter Nichols. *Oddball Sports Yearbook, 2003.*

EXPERIENCE
'If you needed to rewire your house, would you get a brilliant
young electrician to do it, or someone with plenty of experience?'
... veteran trainer Paul Kelleway.

EXPLORERS
'Hardened explorers who have braved obscure tributaries of the
Amazon without batting an eyelid, have turned back in despair
without discovering Goodwood.' ... Peter Oborne on the glorious
adventure of finding the course. *Evening Standard, 31 July 2006*

EXTREMISTS
'The extremists can have their say but the RSPCA is not here to
jump up and down condemning racing' ... David Muir, equine
consultant of the RSPCA, as the row raged over the record number
of equine fatalities at the 2006 Cheltenham Festival. *The Times,
18 March 2006*

EYES
'All my good horses have had good heads, their eyes wide apart.
Do you trust a human when their eyes are too close together?' ...
Henry Cecil, who then widened his theory – 'I never had one good
horse with small ears. The best horses had big ears like Arkle.
Almost like a deer.' *The Sportsman, 14 April 2006*

FABRIC
'Racing was once woven into the fabric of our lives. Even those who did not follow it knew that it mattered.' ... but no more, believes Laura Thompson. *Racing Post, 8 August 2006*

FACE IT
'I must have the sort of face that people like to hit' ... then jockey Jamie Osborne after fellow rider Billy Morris was fined £200 for whacking him and knocking a tooth out in a changing-room row after they had both taken part in a race at Newbury on 28 February 1992; 21 months earlier Jenny Pitman hit him with a right hook.

FAILURE
'It turns out my great grandfather was a failed apprentice jockey who became a groom for most of his working life' ... weather man John Kettley who loves his racing and works with courses, including Cheltenham, predicting what the weather has in store for them. *The Festival, March 2005*

FAINT-HEARTED
'It's not for the faint-hearted, this game. Horses are there to be raced. If you don't want to have a go, don't own racehorses – certainly not with me' ... Mick Channon. *The Times, 20 May 2005*

FALLING IN LOVE
'If you don't want to fall in love with racing, avoid Glorious Goodwood. Don't even watch it on television. If you do, you'll be

hooked as firmly as I was as a child' ... smitten Lydia Hislop. *The Times, 26 July 2005*

'My job is to train them, not fall in love with them' ... Mick Channon, always conscious that his best horses could be moved to Godolphin. *Mail on Sunday, 7 August 2005*

FALLON
'The poet honoured by this colt would have been intrigued by the incongruities of Fallon, by the way he has always thrived on dramas that might finish others off' ... Chris McGrath after Fallon rode Dylan Thomas to win the 2006 Irish Derby. *The Independent, 4 July 2006*

FALLS
'Falls on the Flat happen at greater speed and are never expected, and I believe jockeys should not be allowed to ride again that day, for their safety and the safety of those who are backing their mounts.' ... pro punter Dave Nevison is a bit miffed after Tony Culhane rode a loser he had backed, immediately after taking a hefty fall on Wednesday, 8 December 2004.*Racing & Football Outlook*

'Even the easier falls were taking too long to recover from' ... jockey–turned-trainer Stan Moore on why he packed in the riding. *The Spectator, 26 August 2006*

FANCIED
'I've never asked a trainer if he fancied his runner, because it's really none of my business, and if one has volunteered any info, I've learnt that, more often than not, it isn't helpful' ... Tony Morris. *Pacemaker, July 2006*

FANCY
'Fast youths, fancy men, gamblers, blacklegs and women of easy virtue' ... list of reasons why the *Airdrie Advertiser* wanted local racing banned – in August 1861. Today that could be a list of attractions for certain meetings!

FAREWELL
'Farewell the BBC at Goodwood. How we will miss the presentation team led by Margaret Rutherford and the Clitheroe Kid' ... *Racing Post* reader GC Meek on the end of a fifty year association in August 2006.

FASCISM
'What a pity people don't take as much trouble with their own breeding as intelligent racehorse owners do. But then, I suppose it is bordering on fascism to think like that' ... Jeffrey Bernard, before he was unwell. *The Spectator, 1994.*

FASHION
'What hats are to Ascot, cleavage is to Aintree – without one you are nobody' ... Guardian's Lucy Mangan writing, I suspect, about

ladies at the Grand National meeting in 2005. Her theme was taken up in *The Observer*, quoting a female racegoer asked how to keep warm in the minimum of garments – 'It's easy, just wear two thongs.'

FASTEST
'The way to win a race is to cover the distance in the fastest time. The best way to do that is to run at an even pace' ... it works for Mark Johnston's runners, anyway. *The Spectator, 12 August 2006*

FAST FILLIES
'La Chunga is named after a nightclub in Cannes. We always knew she was a very fast filly, and La Chunga is full of very fast fillies!' ... Barry Simpson, racing manager to Sir Robert Ogden (June 2005).

'I can ride them as fast as they can run' ... US jockey Mary Bacon with a neat putdown of those who doubt the ability and strength of female jockeys. *Racing Post, 12 August 2006*

FATALITY
'How was I supposed to feel, having tried to do a jockey a favour by recommending him for a mount when I learnt the next day that he had been killed in a fall from the beast' ... Tony Morris recalled a sad occasion from his days as a sub editor on the Press Association racing desk. *Racing Post, 25 March 2005*

FATHER, DEAR FATHER
'Horan was prevented from disrupting the start of last year's

Vodafone Derby and, following his behaviour during the Olympics marathon in the summer, we felt that it was in the interest of the safety of horses, riders and 'Father' Horan himself that we took action to prevent him from coming to Epsom Downs for this year's renewal of the Vodafone Derby' ... Stephen Wallis, MD of Epsom on efforts to prevent the controversial cleric, 'Father' Cornelius Horan, from pulling any stunt on 2005 Derby day. *2 June 2005*

FAULTS

'One who sees only the faults of the horse is not necessarily a good judge' ... racing writer John Betts(1945)

FAVOURS

'When I ride in England, the English jockeys don't stop me but they don't do me any favours. It would be the same if an American jockey came to ride France's best horse – the French jockeys would not be happy' ... Christophe Soumillon. *Racing Post, 28 September 2006*

FEAR

'In Britain and Ireland connections of the best horses are paralysed by a fear of being beaten, and what they perceive to be the resulting damage to a horse's reputation'... Nick Luck. *The Sportsman, 4 September 2006*

FEARLESS

'I'd vote for a jockey, fearless speed-merchants ever pressed by

danger, were it not for the ever-present peril of them being lifted from their mount and had up on race-fixing charges' … How others see us? Sue Mott, pondering on her vote for the 2006 BBC TV Sports Personality of the Year Award in August of that year.

'It is a place of fearless bettors and equally fearless bookmakers, a place where the frisson of danger is never far away' … Michael Atherton on the Cheltenham Festival in his 2006 book, *Gambling*.

FESTIVAL FEELINGS
'I went every year but stopped when the course let in so many people that the queues to get to the paddock, to the toilets or into a bar quite simply became unacceptable' … Tony Paley on the Cheltenham Festival. *Racing Ahead, March 2005*

'The best Cheltenham I ever had was when it was off for foot & mouth; it's not been a lucky meeting for me' … Tony Dobbin. *Racing Post, 13 March 2005*

'(Simon) Barnes insists on a special clause in his employment contract to enable him to attend the Cheltenham Festival in its entirety' … Justin O'Regan on former England rugby union international turned writer and broadcaster, Simon Barnes. *The Festival, March 2005*

'An adult Christmas' … Simon Barnes' 1994 description of the Cheltenham Festival.

'**There was an immediate unspoken agreement that neither of us would turn the other one in**' … John Inverdale recalls his first trip to the Festival in 1972, bunking off of school, then bumping into one of his teachers, similarly engaged. *The Festival, March 2005*

'**My friend Kevin and I roared our horse home in the final race, only to find out later it wasn't the beast we'd backed at all. In our defence, they were both brown**' … sports journalist Des Kelly gets over-excited at the 2005 Festival. *Daily Mail, 23 March 2005*

'**We lose one or two customers each year**' … lose, as in 'peg it', 'drop dead', 'pass on', 'go to meet their maker'. Cheltenham Chairman, Lord Vestey, explaining, 'everyone's adrenalin and pulse rises at the moments of high drama at Cheltenham and I'm not surprised one or two keel over.' *Cheltenham, 2005*

'**I'd have to say we now have one day of the Cheltenham Festival and three days building up to it**' … Irish trainer Willie Mullins believes that stretching the Cheltenham Festival to four days has not worked – 'I think the first three days has no spark'. *The Times, 7 February 2007*

'**The only Cheltenham Festival I would ever want to attend is the one staged in the first two weeks of July**' … no jumps fan, Tony Morris, preferring the delights of an 'upmarket celebration of music'. *Racing Post, 25 March 2005*

'An old trout upbraided me as I entered the members' enclosure by insisting that socialists such as me would be happier in the silver ring' ... Robin Cook on the only occasion he has 'been made unwelcome at Cheltenham'. *Guardian, 18 March 2005*

'It is a meeting for the true believers, a proper racing-and-gambling crowd, unlike the social-cum-fashion stakes that characterise some race meetings during the flat season' ... Mike Atherton on Cheltenham in his 2006 book, *Gambling*.

FIGHT
'There were lots of drinking, plenty of shows and towards evening a fight or two, without which to the lower orders a race meeting is a very dull thing indeed' ... no, not a report of a recent Newmarket meeting, but a report in the *New Sporting Magazine* of a meeting at Durham in 1835.

FIRE
'Proceedings were brought to a halt by a fire in somebody's shed. Fire brigade chiefs ruled that the shed was very close to the course and might explode' ... Peter Thomas explains why an Ayr meeting in January 2006 was cancelled.

FIREWORKS
'I know it was suggested by some that she was unsettled by the noise of the fireworks, but that theory isn't the least valid in my opinion' ... trainer Ed Dunlop is not impressed by the excuse offered

by some for the poor display of Ouija Board in the Dubai Sheema Classic at Nad Al Sheba in March 2006 – a race in which some observers were of the opinion that jockey Kieren Fallon had not enjoyed his best ever ride.

FIRST
'I'm due to be in the first race at Goodwood at 2.15pm' ... excuse offered by jockey Neil Callan to the traffic cop who pulled him for speeding at around 100 mph in July, 2005. A year later he received a 12 month dangerous driving ban and a £1,000 fine.

FIRST CLASS
'It attracts 99% of absolutely first class, wonderful people, but I am afraid 1% want to take short cuts, bend the rules and be corrupt' ... Horseracing Regulatory Authority chairman, John Bridgeman. *The Sportsman, 2 April 2006*

FIT
'They are fit for the saddle at foure yeares of age, for the wars at six, for the race at eight, and for hunting or extreme matches, at ten or eleun' ... advice about horses contained in Gervase Marham's 1616 *Medicine for Horses*.

FLIGHT OF FANCY
'David Casey grew up wanting to be a fighter pilot but decided to live dangerously and become a jump jockey instead' *Alan Lee, The Times, 10 March 2005*

FLOORED
'I don't think my Dad realised how hard it was to get a room. We ended up in one room. It had two beds and there were five of us, so someone had to sleep on the floor. The night before the Derby, I did it. I didn't want to be bothered by anybody. I slept like a log' ... Steve Cauthen on his pre-race preparation for winning the 1978 Kentucky Derby on Affirmed.

FOKINE HELL!
'Alice was just mentioning there that the race was won last year by Fokine' ... the gallant Mike Cattermole interjected to spare presenter Alice Plunkett's blushes shortly before Newmarket's King Charles II Stakes in May 2005 as storms played havoc with equipment and she was heard on air complaining that she had 'no f***ing sound'.

FOOD
'I, for one, would resist the temptation to raise the minimum weight as it would be taking food from the mouths of those that need it most' ... Kieren Fallon. *The Sportsman, 15 April 2006*

FOOD CHAIN
'Being low down the food chain you have to live like a sniper – you're not going to get many shots, so you have to make them count!' ... trainer Jon Scargill after his Bobby Charles won at Folkestone in April 2005.

FOOD FOR THOUGHT

'Their kitchens have even got permission for Kosher weddings' ...
Claude Duval reveals an unexpected string to Sandown Park's non-
racing activities. *The Sun, 4 December 2004*

'If someone had told me at the start of the season Beef or Salmon
would be 9/2 for Cheltenham, I'd have assumed it was betting on
the main course in the restaurant' ... William Hill Odds Compiler
Mike Bellamy was shocked to find the Irish raider so prominent in
the betting for the 2006 Gold Cup.

FOOTBALL

'I think some years ago I had the chance of being a Manchester
United or an Arsenal, and I probably did get as far as being a
Tottenham Hotspur, but at best now I vary between an Ipswich
and a Charlton Athletic' ... trainer Luca Cumani modestly assesses
his career progress. *Pacemaker, July 2006*

FOOTBALLERS

'At Arsenal we had a good horse called Go Go Gunner, which I
shared with Peter Marinello, Charlie George and Stan Flashman.
He won races for us, kicking off at Newmarket. There was no
doubt that I was hooked in those days' ... Alan Ball, in his 2004
autobiography, *Playing Extra Time*.

'She walks similar to Jimmy Floyd Hasselbaink – it's all he can do

to get one leg in front of the other' … John Francome's pre-race observation on Channel 4 about 1000 Guineas winner, Attraction.

'When I was playing I used to get away from football by going racing. Now I like to get away from the racing by going to watch football' … ex-footballer and trainer, Mick Quinn. *Daily Mail, 16 December 2004*

FOOTNOTE

'He has to basically re-grow his foot and that's going to take months. If we can keep him comfortable while this is occurring, we have a shot. Horses have re-grown feet before' … Dr Dean Richardson telling the *New York Times* in July 2006 about the condition of Kentucky Derby winner Barbaro, who shattered his leg during the Preakness Stakes and was battling – ultimately unsuccessfully – for survival.

FOREIGNERS

'The "sport" is dependent on needles and painkillers, with several undetectable substances like 'milkshakes' thrown into the equation. The "sameness" of identical left-handed oval racetracks is mind-numbingly boring, and the social climate on most days is like a downmarket dog track' … Julian Wilson is no fan of racing in the States. *Racing Post, 25 October 2005*

'The track was last properly renovated around 1950' … so Vladimir Zhukovskiy, acting director of Russia's Central Moscow

Hippodrome course, knows the amount of work necessary to bring the course up to speed in a bid to attract international entries. *December 2004*

'**Sure, the Poms have Ascot and Frogs have the Arc and the Yanks their Kentucky Derby and Breeders Cup. But nowhere in the world do they have such a grand racetrack party, which lasts a whole week, and gives way to a true Carnival cocktail of colour, culture, coiffure and couture'** … Australia's National Racehorse Owners' Association explaining in November 1995 the appeal of the Melbourne Cup.

'**Hong Kong has the best racing in the world. Every day is a Royal Ascot or a Derby day'** … trainer/owner Ivan Allan. *Racetrack, November 1995*

'**It's a racing paradise here. Trainers don't have to pay bills, send out bills or even collect them. Prize money winnings are credited directly to the trainer's account. It's Shangri-La and I find it more satisfying to be a medium fish in a medium pond than a small fish in a big pond'** … but medium fish are vulnerable to bigger predators, aren't they? Hong Kong-based trainer Ivan Allan. *Racing Review, December 2001*

'**We were hopelessly lost, couldn't read the signs, my French was zero and the locals didn't understand a word I said. All we kept getting was hookers offering all sorts of services!'** … veteran trainer

Milton Bradley on getting lost in the Paris red light district at 3am en route with sprinter The Tatling for the 2004 Prix l'Abbaye in which he finished second. *Mail on Sunday, 5 December 2004*

'There are no owners' colours. Like greyhound racing, the number one wears red, the two white, the three blue and so on. This makes it look like Godolphin has a runner in every race' ... Mary Pitt of BOS magazine on racing at Northampton Fair, Massachusetts were the half-mile around track is tighter than Chester. *December 2004.*

'That's a race I've always wanted to win, but it's in June, which just doesn't suit us' ... trust those dastardly Frenchies to run their Gold Cup at a time unsuitable to Martin Pipe. *The Times, 3 November 2005*

'Young people in the UK have got much bigger. Not enough lightweight people are coming into racing to keep yards properly staffed. We'd be in trouble without the foreign recruits' ... Rupert Arnold, chief executive of the National Trainers' Federation explaining why an estimated 2,500 people from 30 different countries were working in British stables. *News of the World, 27 August 2006*

FOREIGN STUFF
'For me, Dubai racing is the best in the world' ... Syrian-born trainer Mazin Al Kurdi, champion trainer in 2004 of, er, Dubai. *Racing Post, 25 March 2005*

'The smell of horse shit doesn't change much from Europe to America, but from the other side of the course comes the infinitely more fragrant aroma of frying bacon, pancakes and hot coffee' ... Jamie Reid on Lone Star Park in Texas. *Inside Edge, November 2004*

FORM
'Twelve years as a betting shop manager and I thought I'd seen it all. That was until I got asked for the form for Steepledowns!' ... Enfield betting shop manager 'Big' Dave Osborne. *June 2006*

FORM BOOK
'If the form book worked out perfectly all the time there wouldn't be any point in betting' ... Merrick Francis, probably meaning that there wouldn't be any bookies. *Weekend, 3 September 2005*

'I would have known the form book better when I was 10 than I know it now' ... Jeremy Noseda. *Guardian, 9 September 2006*

FRANKIE SPEAKING
'We do not know the real Dettori because we do not live with him. If nothing else, however, his despondency provides him with some captivating depth' ... James Willoughby on Frankie's downbeat reaction to his Dubawi setback when he ignored instructions and lost in the 2005 QEII Stakes, run at Newmarket. *Racing Post, 7 October 2005*

'**Basically, I just did my job by winning another race, but in hindsight it perhaps wasn't the best thing to do. It left a bit of a sour taste with everybody, so perhaps I shouldn't have done it**' ... Frankie Dettori who won the St Leger on Scorpion for rival stable, Coolmore, told R5 Live's Simon Mayo that he wouldn't do it again, in November 2005.

'**When he came to England he was basically a pest and he is still a pest. But he is probably the best rider we've seen in the world for a very, very long time**' ... Luca Cumani on Frankie, who had just ridden his Alkaased to win the 2005 Japan Cup.

'**When you're into gambling like that every day and hooked on it, it really is better than sex. It takes you somewhere else, it makes your heart go faster.**' ... Frankie quoted in the January 2006 edition of *Inside Edge* remembering his earlier days when he was in to punting.

'**I wouldn't be happy if they said they wanted to be jockeys**' ... Frankie on his kids. *Daily Express, 27 November 2006*

FREEDOM
'**Wales has done nothing for me. They gave Norton's Coin the freedom of Carmarthen – but not me**' ... Sirrell Griffiths, trainer of shock 100/1 Cheltenham Gold Cup winner Norton's Coin. *Racing Post, 9 March 2007*

FRESH
'After going to stud and covering 60 mares you would be a bit fresh, wouldn't you?' ... Aidan O'Brien is happy enough with George Washington's comeback run having been at stud.

FROSTY RECEPTION
'Well, dear boy, the first thing you do is start praying for frost' ... J A McGrath of the *Daily Telegraph* recalls the response by Hugo Bevan, clerk of the course at Windsor, Towcester, Huntingdon and Worcester simultaneously, when asked what happened when more than one were due to race on the same day.

FUN
'Racing is the best fun you can have with your clothes on' ... Robin Oakley. *Spectator Guide to Cheltenham, 2006*

FUNDAMENTAL
'The fact that a lot of paying spectators have no clear view of racing is about as fundamental as it gets' ... Alan Lee cuts to the chase about the 'new' Ascot's glaring problem. *The Times, 14 August 2006*

FURLONG POLE
'I'd rather have Darryl Holland than any other jockey at the furlong pole' ... Mark Johnston. *The Sun, 17 December 2005*

FURS

'Like a posh point-to-point with furs instead of Barbours' ... Alan Lee reports Mark Johnston's view on racing on ice at St Moritz. *The Times, 21 February 2006*

FUSS

'It's a bit like Royal Ascot, but with less fuss and more chasers' ... David Ashforth on the Galway Festival. *Racing Post, 4 August 2006*

GAMBLING

'I got the impression that it was the gambling rather than the horses that he liked' ... Detective Steve Daniels on Graham Price, from Swansea, who stole £10m, much of which he gambled, even reportedly spending a seven figure sum on tipsters. *Evening Standard, 8 November 2005*

GANG BANG

'If they have a gang-bang at the two-mile marker there's not much we can do about it' ... bizarre comment by Newmarket steward Leslie Harrison, about the long-running 3m 6f Newmarket Town Plate during which the runners go out of view for some three minutes, won on 27 August 2006 by 12-year-old Papua.

GARDEN PARTY

'A garden party with racing tacked on' ... King Edward VII's description of racing at Goodwood in the early 20th century.

GAUNTLET

'His death will be felt most in the weighing room, not least because every one of them knows that the daily gauntlet they run means it could have been them' ... Alastair Down, paying tribute to 20-year-old jump jockey Tom Halliday, killed at Market Rasen in July 2005.

GAY

'I was born at a time when gay meant happy, clap meant applause and only generals had aides' ... former amateur rider, owner and trainer Gay Kindersely, in February 2007.

GENUINE

'I don't think there is such an animal as a racehorse that is not genuine. If they don't give their all, you can bet your life there is something amiss with them and as the trainer, it's your job to find out what it is' ... Mick Channon, 2004

GENIUS

'McCoy has won more races than anyone ever, but if Richard Johnson had been Martin Pipe's stable jockey for the past eight years, or Mick Fitzgerald, or even Seamus Durack, might we not be celebrating their genius rather than McCoy's?' ... thought provoking comment in *Oddball Sports Yearbook 2003*.

'The supreme artist plying his craft from the saddle, his genius as sublime as that of a Rembrandt or a Beethoven, and his

accomplishments on the same plane' … so, experienced racing journalist Tony Morris is a fan of Lester Piggott, to judge by the comment made after his Derby victory on Teenoso.

'A trainer is only as good as his owners. You may think you're a genius, but you try and be a genius without any horses. I went from swimming along quite nicely to drowning' … Paul Cole thinks back to the death of his chief owner Fahd Salman in 2001. *Racing Post, 10 September 2006*

GET LOST
'It's a tough old road in this game and we've all got lost on the way. If I helped him, that's great, but it would have been awful if we'd lost him because he has such quality' … Kieren Fallon on helping title challenging jockey Robert Winston put his career back on the rails after drink-related problems. *The Times, 21 July 2005*

GETTING THEIR PRIORITIES RIGHT
'Demand Democracy Now' – the slogan on the front of the pantomime horse fancy dress worn by a protestor at the 2004 Hong Kong Cup meeting, whose action in running on to the track reportedly 'angered connections' of British raider, Rakti. At least they were at liberty to express their disapproval freely.

GHASTLY
'Because of ghastly events in the wider world, Epsom has been abandoned this evening' … tragic reason for the cancellation of

Epsom's 7 July 2005 meeting, explained by Alastair Down on Channel 4, following the terrorist attack on the tube and buses that morning.

GIANT NIPPLE
'My wife was outside after the trophy presentation and some guy walked up with a giant nipple on his head, like a hat. He asked her how everything went. She said we had a great day and won the race. He said "Oh, really? That's nice" Then went on his way' … trainer John Ward Jr on the aftermath of his Monarchos' 2001 Kentucky Derby win, explaining how some people just make tits of themselves.

GIFT
'Victoria thinks I'm lucky, that I have some sort of gift like a water diviner' … Anthony Pakenham explains why horses owned by him and wife Victoria race in his colours. And she just may have a point. They own Derby winner, Sir Percy. *Pacemaker, July 2006*

GIRLFRIEND
'Selecting a horse is like finding a girlfriend; you have to love them at first sight because you're seeing them at 6.30 every morning' … trainer Ben Pollock – married to Nicola – in February 2006.

GIRLY
'She is the best woman jockey I have seen' … Alastair Down on Nina Carberry. *Racing Post, 16 March 2005*

'Carrie is a grand lass, but she's a brood mare now and having kids does not get you fit to ride Grand Nationals' ... Ginger McCain unimpressed with fancied Forest Gunner's partner for the 2005 National, Ms Ford, adding, 'Horses do not win Grand Nationals ridden by women. That's a fact.' *Daily Mail, 23 March 2005*

'If it was me and I won the race, I'd go up to him and say "kiss my arse"' ... Royal Ascot-winning jockey-turned-trainer Gay Kelleway with some bum advice for Carrie Ford. *Guardian, 1 April 2005*

'If you ride round there having just given birth, believe me that's showing more bottle than most men have got' ... Jenny Pitman supports Ms Ford, who won over the Aintree fences in 2004, ten weeks after having daughter Hannah. *Racing Post, 25 March 2005*

'I know it might disappoint some people, but I'm not an advocate of the view that women can compete on any horse. Men will always have the strength and some horses need that' ... Carrie Ford. *Guardian, 1 April 2005*

'When I picked up the *Racing Post* and saw Carrie's face on it, I thought 'thank goodness I married a pretty bird' ... Carrie's husband, Richard.

'The path for women jockeys can be narrower than for the men – there are more rocks on our path, but there is a path' ... superstar US jockey, Julie Krone. *Guardian, 1 April 2005*

'In the skill stakes they are as adept as men and can squeeze more out of certain mounts' ... Peter Scudamore on the riding talents of Lisa Jones and Hayley Turner. *Daily Mail, 30 March 2005*

'I'm not sure how long it's going to take for a female to break through at the top level in Britain, because there's no real tradition of it here' ... one of the best female riders here, Alex Greaves on Lisa Cropp's achievement in August 2005 of becoming champion New Zealand jockey with a record 197 wins.

GIVE UP
'I don't want to give up by being made to give up' ... Henry Cecil, before his stunning Classic-winning comeback in 2007. *The Independent, 29 May 2005*

GLIDERS
'It was like Arnhem all over again' ... steward's secretary Geoff Forster after four gliders landed unexpectedly on the airstrip alongside the course at Newmarket's 26 August 2005 meeting.

GLORIOUS
'There is a holiday atmosphere about the whole meeting and the women appear at their best, and shine far more brilliantly that at Ascot where they walk about with the formality and stiffness of a registered parcel' ... Ascot compared unfavourably with Glorious Goodwood in the 1952 *Racing Review Annual* – plus ça change!

GLORY

'There's nothing to beat the sight of horses in their thoroughbred prime thundering past the finishing-post to glory' ... unexpected declaration by Sandra Howard, wife of former Tory leader, Michael. *Stella, 24 September 2006*

GODS

'There used to be a lot of old trainers, all in their 70s, and the local townspeople thought they were gods. They didn't pay their bills because they were too good to pay bills' ... Michael Jarvis on how it was when he first trained in Newmarket. *Racing Post, 27 May 2005*

'We took well into six figures and made a profit, which just goes to show that God is a bookie' ... Paddy Power finance director Ross Ivers on his company's market on the 2005 Papal election. *The Times, 1 September 2005*

'Dunno, how old is God?' ... Nigel Twiston-Davies in September 2005, on being asked how long Carl Llewellyn had ridden for him.

GOING NOT SO GOOD

'Nobody seems to have any idea where the horses are going next – including the jockeys' ... Simon Milham is convinced that Cheltenham's Cross Country Handicap Chase is 'something of a blot on the landscape'. *Pacemaker, March 2005*

'It's the worst ground I've ever ridden on anywhere in the world'
… Kieren Fallon on Deauville after the 2005 Prix Morny (in which he was beaten on Ivan Denisovich) in August.

GOLDEN MOMENT
'It was like the trophy was going back home. It made my day' … Jonny Frais from Newcastle who sold the 1958 Cheltenham Gold Cup trophy won by Kerstin for £8,110 on eBay in March 2005 – to a 92-year-old man who told him he had sold the horse to trainer George H Moore.

GOLF
'I play off 13 and when I play with the pros they make me want to throw my clubs in the corner. But then I think: "They're not very good on a horse". And I feel better' … Mick Fitzgerald on playing golf. *The Times, 21 September 2006*

GONE MISSING
'We have mislaid Luke Harvey' … Rachel Burden on Radio Five Live on the non-appearance of the former jockey turned publican cum pundit, for his 6.55am racing slot on Saturday, 11 December 2004.

GON WOBBLY
'Tony got down on one to knee to propose, even though the gondola was a bit wobbly' … an anonymous 'friend' reporting on

how Tony McCoy proposed to partner Chanelle Burke whilst afloat in Venice. *Daily Mail, 22 July 2005*

GOOD

'I soon knew he was a good horse because I've got so many bad ones' ... trainer Robin Bastiman on stable star, Borderlescott. *The Spectator, 12 August 2006*

'Good women, good horses and good jockeys find you. You don't have to go looking for them' ... Harvey Smith, who should know! *Racing Post, 30 August 2006*

GOOD BREEDING

'I've studied every book there is on breeding and, when I was growing up, my bible was the Bobinski table of families' ... so there! Prominent French owner and breeder Alec Wildenstein knows his stuff. *Pacemaker, March 2005*

GOON

'He's a big goon and he'll fall over himself if you give him the chance' ... trainer Bryan Smart is not over impressed with the coordination of his April 2006 Free Handicap at Newmarket winner Misu Bond who, he seems to believe, has a certain resemblance to Spike Milligan, Harry Secombe, Peter Sellers and/or Michael Bentine.

GRANDSTAND

'This is really one of those buildings where the best view is from in

it: a clumpy, Frankenstein agglomeration of pitched roofs, folksy
dormers and faux Victorian conservatories that appear to have
suffered a fatal attack of Supermarket Vernacular. An overblown
confection resembling a mutant cricket pavilion' ... well, do you
think Catherine Slessor, who wrote this in the 1994 Architectural
Review, actually liked Newbury's new Berkshire Grandstand?

GRASSED UP
'I was so desperately disappointed when Dancing Brave was
beaten in the Derby, I took my frustration out to the garden to
mow the lawn. That wasn't enough to change my mood, so I
mowed my neighbour's lawn, and by the time I'd finished that
night I'd cut every blade of grass on the estate' ... former jockey
Chris Kinane, recovering from being kicked in the head by a horse,
recalled one of his most memorable days in racing, when he was
assistant to Guy Harwood. *Racing Post, 11 July 2006*

GREATEST
'The greatest race in the history of Flat racing' ... Brough Scott's
Channel 4-related opinion in February 2005 of the Arc de Triomphe
won by Dancing Brave, whose jockey Pat Eddery had declared that
he would 'hold him up a bit' before executing a masterful first to last
swoop.

'Sheikh Mohammed is the greatest thing to ever hit this business.
His outfit isn't trying to make a dollar on the thing and they're
spreading the money around everywhere. They're educating kids

and creating jobs. Just thank God he loves thoroughbred
racehorses and not something else' ... Consignor John Stuart of
Bluegrass Thoroughbred Services. *Racing Post, 15 September 2005*

GREAT ONES
'I think that was the best race ever' ... Moscow Flyer's ecstatic
owner Brian Kearney may have slightly over-stated the victory over
Azertyuiop in Sandown's December 2004 Tingle Creek Chase but I
and the other 16,300 who were there wouldn't argue too much with
his assessment.

'I didn't even know if he was a horse or a cow' ... at the age of
two, trainer Tom Taaffe got to sit on a horse for the first time – one
ridden by his dad, Pat – one called Arkle. *The Independent,
7 December 2004*

GREEDY
'The bodies running the sport are simply greedy. The authorities
should share the responsibilities and take the initiative. What is
wrong with declaring a blank day each week and giving everyone a
day off?' ... leading jockeys' agent, Shippy Ellis argues against
possible jockey burn-out through over-work and dehydration.
23 June 2005

GREY
'I remember driving home after Kalypso Katie's Oaks, and the
whole world seemed grey. I got up the next morning, and I felt like

I'd lost a member of my family or something. It's stupid, but that's what it means to me' ... Jeremy Noseda, who doesn't like losing. *Guardian, 9 September 2006*

GRIEF
'They take it in turns' ... said Ayr, Musselburgh and Perth clerk of the course Anthea Morshead, when asked 'who gives you more grief – owners, trainers or jockeys?'

'Some of the stuff I've seen on the internet reminds me of the astounding outpouring of grief in Britain that accompanied the death of Princess Diana. At least she was human' ... Nicholas Godfrey is uneasy at the emotions released following the death of Kentucky Derby winner Barbaro after his leg was shattered in the Preakness Stakes and a nation followed his ultimately tragic fight for life. *Racing Post, 4 February 2007*

GRIT
'In Britain, once a horse has run over hurdles, even if he's won on the Flat, he's labelled National Hunt. In France, they say, "here is a horse who had the speed to win on the Flat and also showed the grit and determination to win over jumps", and they take it as a bonus. Until the Flat look at it that way here, we're never going to have Flat stallions covering National Hunt mares as well' ... Peter Hockenhull of Shade Oak Stud, Britain's foremost NH stud. *Racing Post, 30 March 2007*

GUIDING
'I once met a stud farm worker who described what he did as 'guiding'. This wasn't, as I thought, showing people around the farm. He acted as a tour guide for an altogether different client. It could be said that he had his hands full in more ways than one' ... Jack Houghton, Betfair communications manager. *The Sportsman, 2 August 2006*

GUINEAS
'Am I the only one who thinks that selling horses in Guineas is outdated, elitist nonsense?' ... no traditionalist, former champion jockey Richard Dunwoody. *Daily Mirror, 26 May 2007*

GUILTY
'I still feel a bit guilty' ... Sir Clement Freud, confessing in November 2005 that in 1951 he knowingly accepted an over-payment for his Tote bet on Colonist at Royal Ascot, for which he received £123 when 'I was expecting £9.' *Racing Post, 23 November 2005*

HAMFISTED
'Of all the hamfisted rules that have come in, this must be the best ... It's health and safety gone mad' ... Clive Brittain is unhappy about new rules banning the exercising of racehorses in the dark at Newmarket. *Racing Post, 23 July 2007*

HANDICAP

'In a time when British racing is being scrutinized more closely than ever, surely a system in which handicaps are contested by horses whose real ability can only be guessed at by punters, cannot be credible?' ... Darryl Sherer, Editor of *Pacemaker*, suggesting that some horses contest handicaps when their true ability can only be guessed at. *September 2006*

HANDICAPPING

'It's been an oft heard but, in my view, unfounded gripe in recent years that horses are as likely to be handicapped on who trains them as their ability' ... Marten Julian. *Racing Post, 3 July 2005*

'It will normally take me five or six goes before I finally come up with one that works. I'll spend a whole day on one sometimes and then I'll realise that it's not working and I just have to rip it up and start again' ... Grand National handicapper, Phil Smith, who also said of the reaction to his work – 'I'd hope that everyone is a little disappointed. I'm not there for compliments. I'm there to make sure all the horses have got an equal chance.' *Guardian, 2 February 2006*

'If the Irish ever complain about handicapping again I'll kill them' ... Nicky Henderson is less than pleased at the 2006 Cheltenham Festival when his runners are narrowly foiled by Irish raider Dun Doire in the William Hill Chase.

'I should like to see horses handicapped from the bottom, not the top, and every horse's saliva should be tested after winning' ... interesting 1961 pleas by Yorkshire jumps trainer Charles Wood, who also complained 'Small trainers like myself do not get a chance with the handicapper.' Forty five years later support for his opinion was offered in the *Racing Post* of 15 September 15 2006 when trainer Norma Macauley suggested, 'It is high time we had upside down handicaps in order to give the smaller owners and trainers a chance of a runner.'

'The authorities are obsessed with integrity and spend huge amounts of time and money trying to maintain it, while operating a handicap system which encourages and often rewards "cheating"' ... Mark Johnston makes his opinion crystal clear and adds 'I don't believe there should be handicap racing at all'. *Pacemaker, October 2006*

HANDKERCHIEF
'I call him the handkerchief because he's always in a pocket' ... pundit Tom Segal on jockey Jamie Spencer. *Weekender, 23 July 2006*

HANDY
'She wants me to insure my hands in case I get hurt when I'm riding. I've already knocked myself out five times, so it might be a good idea' ... Nichola Eddery, daughter of jockeys Pat and Carolyn, who still rides out but earns her living from her racing paintings which go for four figure sums. *The Times, 9 June 2005*

HANGERS ON
'The hangers-on are the weeds of the Turf and thrive just as easily'
… racing writer John Betts in 1946.

HAPPENSTANCE
'Atkinson is the only rider who I ever heard use the word "happenstance"' … tribute by an un-named journalist to the vocabulary of US jockey Ted Atkinson who died on 5 May 2005, aged 88.

HAPPY
'When I win a race I'm too happy, and people who lost are not happy because they see I'm so happy' … looking for a happy medium, Christophe Soumillon. *Racing Post, 28 September 2006*

HAPPY BIRTHDAY
'I was christened in a small Catholic church in Kent and there must have been a mistake. There is absolutely no doubt about it – I was born on 29 July (in 1948)' … insisted Irish trainer Dermot Weld after the *Racing Post*'s John Randall came across a birth certificate giving his date of birth as 29 February

HARDEST
'I've had 16 companies, in demolition, waste disposal and others, and training racehorses is the hardest job of the lot. It's seven days a week, Christmas, New Year's day. I haven't been away in years' … Terry Mills loves training, really. *Racing Post, July 2006*

HARRODS
'While he never shopped in Harrods he had no problems getting Harrods results' ... early 2005 tribute by Ted Walsh to retiring trainer Paddy Mullins.

HASSLE
'To win the title would bring too much hassle, and when we lost it people would say we'd gone at the game' ... trainer Philip Hobbs explains why he is happy to allow others to battle it out up front. *Racing Post, 11 October 2005*

HATTER
'He's a brilliant bloke, but mad as a hatter. He knows everything there is to know about racing, but ask him how to put on a kettle and he wouldn't have a clue' ... jockey Duran Fentiman, on working with Michael Dickinson. *Racing Post, 24 April 2005*

'Order was eventually restored by police, but not before many were injured, 26 so seriously they had to be admitted to hospital' ... and what heinous incident had sparked the virtual riot at Sha Tin racecourse in Hong Kong, described by Paul Haigh in April 2005? The giving away to a crowd of 50,000, a total of just 10,000 baseball caps named after local equine hero, Silent Witness.

'Wearing at one point a very amusing wide-brimmed blue hat which I think may have been modelled on the spacecraft out of Close Encounters of the Third Kind, although possibly not playing

the tune' ... Martin Kelner admires Clare Balding's millinery creation at the 2005 Derby. *6 June 2005*

HAVING IT OFF
'At one time I was told it might have to come off' ... jockey Steve Wynne recalled the potential consequence of an accident to his leg at Haydock on 16 December 1995.

'If ever anyone hears of someone "having it off" at Southwell, it may not be a betting coup to which they are referring' ... *Racing Post* columnist The Dikler reporting that a condom machine has been installed in the jockeys' changing room at Southwell. *Racing Post, 12 July 2006*

HEAD BUTTING
'Gentleness is the way of the strong-minded horseman. Head-butting is the way of the wimp' ... Simon Barnes on the controversial incident in which jockey Paul O'Neill head-butted his mount, City Affair. *The Times, 26 July 2006*

'Sure, pushing your forehead into the face of a horse is an abysmal act, especially when you have a helmet on. Is it any worse, though, than repeatedly smashing it over the arse with a whip when it is absolutely knackered to get it to decelerate a bit less suddenly?' ... Bruce Millington. *Racing Post, 26 July 2006*

HEALTHY

'I know for a fact that I'm not going to be healthy when I'm 60 – the doctors have told me. They are concerned about my bones – I broke a leg and it took six months to heal – and I am constantly dehydrated and get back trouble' ... jockey Richard Hughes on the cost of wasting to make the weight. *Racing Post, 16 April 2006*

HEAT OF THE MOMENT

'He absolutely pissed it' ... is what I am absolutely convinced I heard trainer Tom Taaffe tell TV viewers after Kicking King had won the 2005 Cheltenham Gold Cup, followed by 'it was the horse who told me he wanted to come here'

HIGH CLASS

'High class trainers prepare their two-year-olds inwardly; their three-year-olds outwardly' ... racing writer John Betts in 1945.

HIGH HEELS

'My penetrometers are my high heels' ... Deirdre Johnston revealed how she had decided the ground was right for flying filly Attraction, a September 2005 winner at Leopardstown.

HIGH PRAISE

'Lester Piggott, Yves St Martin, Steve Cauthen – and Julien Leparoux. Every twenty or thirty years, a new one comes along and I have no doubt whatsoever that Leparoux is far better than all of the other jockeys I have helped form. People come up to me

MASKED WRESTLING
'Horseracing appears far from fascinating to the average sports mad Mexican, a long way down the list of priorities behind football, bullfighting and, of all things, masked wrestling' ... Nicholas Godfrey, about Mexico, currently boasting just one race track. *Racing Post, 29 May 2005*

MASSAGE
'I can't tell you much about how good the filly was, it's the part the wife will have to massage tonight that I am worried about' ... Seb Sanders, quoted by trainer Clive Brittain after his saddle slipped whilst partnering Extreme Beauty to victory at Yarmouth in July 2005.

MASTER
'Nobody wants to win as badly as he does. He's an absolute master of his craft, like none before' ... Aidan O'Brien on Kieren Fallon. *The Independent, 15 July 2006*

MASTERMIND
'If I was to appear on Mastermind, Flat racing would have to be my specialist subject. It is also likely to be my career once I have finished scoring goals' ... but not, one imagines, in terms of becoming a jockey. England striker Michel Owen on his love of the sport. *The Times, 16 January 2006*

MEATY MATTER
'Make sure there's plenty of expensive meat in the arse of them, because that's where the power comes from' ... trainer of 1970 Whitbread winner Royal Toss, Tim Handel's advice recalled by owner Arnold Sendell.

MEDIA MOAN
'Racing journalists are, in my opinion, far too close to the trainers and jockeys they should be judging and as a result the racing public is done a disservice' ... *Racing Post* letter writer, William Wall from Edgbaston. *Racing Post, 23 March 2005*

'Racing press rooms are strange places. They are filled with obsessives and aficionados trading information' ... I'm not quite sure into which camp Will Buckley of *The Observer* who made this observation in April 2005, fits.

MEDIOCRE
'I hate mediocre people. I just don't take the time to talk to them. When I go racing it is to work. I don't have the time to say hello' ... reticent French trainer Andre Fabre. Oh well, I didn't really want to talk to him anyway.

'All the mediocre racecourses should be phased out and there should be 15 really good courses' ... so that would have been Julian Wilson's 1988 idea of really good courses, then.

MEMORIES

'Persian Punch was everything that you could possibly dream about in a racehorse. It is sad he has gone, but the memories will live on forever' ... owner Jeff Smith pays tribute to the great horse, of whom a bronze statue was unveiled at Newmarket on October 15, 2005.

'What are they, these races that flower with each summer, but a quest for greatness? What are we hoping for when we watch them, but a glimpse of a horse whose memory will live for us forever?' ... or, perhaps, more prosaically, a winner? Laura Thomspon, from her 1996 book, *Quest For Greatness*.

MENTAL

'We've got her on a magnesium based product which they apparently give to mental patients. She really is a witch in her box' ... trainer Pat Sly on her August 2005 Beverley and future Classic-winner Speciosa.

MENTAL STRENGTH

'I'm not mentally strong enough to handle the excitement of a day like this' ... poignant comment from soon-to-retire David Loder, who was at Newmarket, when his 14/1 shot Goodricke won the William Hill Sprint Cup at Haydock on 3 September 2005.

MERITS

'It's the first time in 35 years that it has been suggested that a

horse of mine has not been run on its merits' ... complained trainer Dave Thom on 29 February 1995 after his Tiger Shoot, running at Southwell, became the first horse to be banned under the non-trier rules. He was fined £1000 and the horse banned from racing for thirty days.

MILKING IT
'For many years we did a milk round in the village, the wife and I. We'd get up early, milk the cows, do out round and then go racing. When we got home we'd do the evening milking, too' ... Eric Alston, who joined the cream of trainers in August 2006 at the age of 62 when his Reverence won the Group One, Nunthorpe Stakes.

MIND OF HIS OWN
'He's good, and he knows he's good...It's like a game of chess with him all the time. He night do anything and if you make the wrong move, you'll upset him and that's it for the day' ... Philip Robinson on the enigmatic Rakti. *Sunday Times, 12 June 2005*

MISERABLE
'I was treated like slave labour. Gwilt was a right ba*tard, a miserable old sod, and he never gave apprentices rides' ... 1946/47 champion jump jockey Jack Dowdeswell was still bitter about his five year stay with Lambourn trainer Ted Gwilt when he was celebrating his 90th birthday in May 2007 .

MISTAKE
'The man who never makes a mistake is not a man' … Michael Hourigan, whose Hi Cloy won the Paddy Power Chase at Leopardstown on 27 December, 2005 after Central House's jockey Roger Loughran, stood up to celebrate when in front on the run-in – but had mistaken the whereabouts of the winning post.

MOB
'Better than Ascot. That's for the elite. This is racing for the mob and they love it' … Bookmaker David Pipe, father of trainer Martin, welcomed the arrival of floodlit racing at Wolverhampton in 1994.

MODERN
'The biggest mistake that racing in general has made is to try to be modern' … traditionalist Charlie Brooks. *Daily Telegraph, 31 July 2006*

MODESTY
'I hope I train so long that I can't remember anything' … Arc winning trainer Michael Jarvis, aged 66, down-playing suggestions of an autobiography. *Pacemaker April 2005*, and dismissing his career as a jockey: 'I had three winners jumping and wasn't terribly good.'

'The average racegoer's modest ambition is to find a place from which the opportunities to eat, drink, watch the race and urinate

are no more than a minute away' ... Sir Clement Freud *Racing Post, 31 May 2006*

MONEY

'In horse racing if you don't turn up for a race you don't get any money and what you earn depends on how many wins you have' ... former jockey, Willie Carson, chairman of Swindon FC, explaining why he is disillusioned by soccer, where 'people are given huge contracts, paid what they want and earn the same money even if they don't play and end up spending most of their time in bed.' *The League Paper, 23 October 2005*

'I did a Cheltenham game last night, and when I came away I realised it was the first time I'd ever left Cheltenham with some money in my pocket' ... gambling journeyman footballer turned commentator Steve Claridge. *Radio Five Live, 18 May 2006*

'What would you do with the money? Spend it all buying lots more horses and never find one half as good as the one you've sold' ... owner Anthony Pakenham explaining why he and wife Victoria turned down huge offers for their horse which had just won a £2500 Goodwood maiden. Sir Percy went on to win the 2006 Derby.

'I say to owners that you don't expect to make money out of your other hobbies, like your golfing holidays, your skiing trips, your boats or your mistress, so you shouldn't expect to make money out of owning racehorses' ... Luca Cumani. *Pacemaker, July 2006*

MONKEY BUSINESS

'Carla Moore, race planning executive and I spot a monkey in a tree while walking our dogs on Ascot's Old Mile at lunchtime, and report it to a bemused policeman' ... work-rider and RCA communication and sponsorship executive, reports a real monkey puzzle. *Racing Post, 3 August 2005*

'He's a monkey, so we brought him to a monkey track and its worked' ... trainer Brett Johnson on how his August 2005 winner Treetops Hotel came to take part in his race at Brighton.

'In the mutuel machines, a monkey gets the same price as a man' ... racegoer E Phocian Howard, expressing his disapproval of the 1940 introduction of pari mutuel gambling to New York, outlawing bookmakers.

MORALITY MATTERS

'Sporting moralists can only hope that the cordial evidence of chivalry after every race at Cheltenham this week might somehow transfer to the wooden numbskulls of some watching Premiership footballers' ... Frank Keating. *The Guardian, 18 March 2005*

MORRIS DANCING

'Never get involved in incest, Morris dancing, or betting odds-on' ... advice from his Dad to racing writer Claude Duval. *The Sun, 3 June 2006*

MORTALITY

'He had the blanket of roses over his neck. His head was hanging a bit, his ears were pricked up and he had mud all over his face. It made him look mortal, and I thought he was almost immortal. You could see he gave it all, and he was tired. It made him look so humble' ... trainer John Servis on his 2004 Kentucky Derby winner, Smarty Jones.

MOSES

'Moses himself could not unite the racing industry; it is composed of many factional interests, some of which co-exist at each other's expense' ... James Willoughby. *Racing Post, 25 January 2006*

MULTI-CULTURAL

'Oh to be at Epsom in the baking heat on multi-cultural Derby day. Musicians, chavs, spivs, Arabs (bit thin on the ground), Irishmen, Jews, Muslims, long-faced Frenchmen, geisha girls on stilts, threadbare aristocrats, Indians, the odd mayor, quite jovial policemen and Anglo-Saxons behaving to stereotype as they drank too much while the sun beat down on them. And that was just in the owners and trainers section' ... Charlie Brooks on the 2006 Derby day scene. *Daily Telegraph, 5 June 2006*

MUSIC

'The New Seekers' ... Derek Thompson's choice of 'Music' in a *Sportsman* interview, 21 August 2006.

MYSTICAL

'It is as if Vincent can see not only into the yearling's heart and lungs but into his brain, into his character and thus, by definition, into his future. It is magical, almost mystical to watch' ... from *Vincent O'Brien, the Official Biography* by Jacqueline O'Brien and Ivor Herbert. No hero worship there, then.

MYSTIQUE

'Most people do view a day's racing as something special. They like its traditions, its dress codes, its mystique – all the things that have been confused with elitism, but in fact have far more to do with racing's glorious ability to take us into a different world' ... Laura Thompson. *Racing Post, 29 June 2006*

NAFF

'In some ways, letting everyone in free was an admission that we were a naff track with poor facilities' ... obviously, though, Chris Palmer, Towcester racecourse chief executive, only got round to admitting this when he announced that they would in future be charging a fiver a time to get in from October, 2005. *The Times, 1 September 2005*

NAME GAME

'The name obviously got through the system, but when it surfaced at the entry stage the stewards said 'we can't be doing with this'' ... Jockey Club spokesman David Pipe, explaining why a horse due to run at Folkestone on Monday, March 27, 1995 was threatened with withdrawal unless its name was changed – from Wear The Fox Hat. The two year old filly, owned by Newmarket farmer Julian Wilson (not THAT one) eventually turned out as Nameless.

'Heartthrob was taken so I thought about my riding and training for all those years and called him Heartache' ... owner/trainer/breeder of Towcester chase winner in January 2006, Robin Matthew explains how the horse got its name.

THE NATIONAL

'Mythic' ... French trainer Guillaume Macaire's succinct description of the National.

'This race is not actually taking place' ... racecourse commentator during 1993 Grand National which never was, 'won' by Esha Ness.

'By the end there were far more BBC commentators than horses' ... Clive James on the four finisher 1980 National.

'Its inherent dangers reinforce the notion that racing's central appeal is the trade-off of safety for thrills' ... James Willoughby on the Grand National. *Pacemaker, April 2005*

'One of the ways I justify the National to myself is that if a horse doesn't want to compete he pulls up' ... Sir Peter O'Sullevan. *The Independent, 4 April 2005*

'In the 166 years since it was first run it is possible to argue that the Grand National has finally become the race it was always intended to be. This is, in its way, a more competitive race than 1929 when a record 66 runners went to post. The days when 30 of the 40 runners effectively went to post without any chance at all have been consigned to history' … Greg Wood welcomes a classier National. *The Guardian, 9 April 2005*

'If I could win just one more race, I would choose the National again. I didn't appreciate it enough the first time around' … Tony Dobbin, celebrating his 1,000th winner on Alfy Rich at Hexham in October 2005, recalls his 1997 National triumph on Lord Gyllene.

'If we are honest, the principal reason why we find the Grand National so exciting is that there are always so many fallers' … Bruce Anderson. But far from wanting the race scrapped because of this, Anderson declares: 'In order for the race to retain its glory and its terror, it is important that a horse should be killed most years and a jockey every ten years or so.' *The Times, 7 April 2006*

NATIONALITY
'Most French, after years of conveniently forgetting Soumillon is Belgian, are now reminding everyone of his nationality' … French-based *Racing Post* reader Ann Eckelberry after Soumillon's bizarre 'kiss my bum' gestures following his 2006 King George win on Hurricane Run.

NATIONAL PASTIME
'The history of horse racing as detailed will have shown that the sport is one which, from antiquity of custom and its being particularly suited to the nature of an Englishman, gives it a pre-eminent claim to be considered the national pastime of the people' ... anonymous author of 1863's *Horse Racing*.

NEXT ARKLE ?
'When this horse won his first bumper, my first son was born. We named him Pat and, jokingly, we said, "now we've found the new Pat Taaffe, we've just got to find the next Arkle"' ... and 'this horse' Kicking King duly did the business when he won the 2005 Cheltenham Gold Cup, eliciting this response from trainer Tom Taaffe.

NERVES
'When I was riding I never got nervous, whether it was the Gold Cup or a selling hurdle. But training them is a whole lot different. When they go out to race it's all out of your hands and I was a bag of nerves today' ... Adrian Maguire after Hardwick gave him his first Listowel Festival winner on 21 September 2005.

NEWS
'If he wins I think it will be front-page news, or maybe back-page news because we read the other way from you' ... Japanese horse Heart Cry's trainer Kojiro Hashiguchi before his runner finished 3rd in the 2006 King George at Ascot.

NICE
'It's nice to be important, but it's more important to be nice' … refreshing, if a little twee, sentiment from Best Mate's jockey, Jim Culloty. *The Festival, March 2005*

'Everyone I've met in racing has been nice, charming and happy to talk freely with me. It's the complete opposite to what I had for all those years in business' … really! I wonder why racing folk would want to be so nice to the billionaire-owner Graham Wylie? Cheltenham 2005.

NICKNAME
'The grown-up Milky Bar Kid' … Mark Winstanley on Aidan O'Brien. *Weekender, 4 May 2005*

'Believe it or not he's proud to be the hairiest jockey on the circuit and rejoices in that nickname' … Carl Llewellyn reveals weighing-room colleague Seamus Durack's nickname of 'Baboon' – also shopping Ollie McPhail who, 'from a certain angle, he may look a bit like a Pork Pie.' *Racing Post, 26 August 2005*

NIGHTMARE
'Goodwood is always a nightmare, especially when you have a good horse to ride' … Kieren Fallon is not over-keen on the glorious Sussex track. *The Times, 26 July 2005*

NON TRIER

'I can't believe I've come here to ride a non-trier when I could have gone to Ripon for five good things' ... 'cock o'the north' top jockey of the day, Eddie Hide, at Epsom on Derby Day to ride trainer Arthur Budgett's Projector – on whom he'd just been told 'not to give him too hard a race as he'd been backward' recalled the trainer, whose Morston promptly won the Classic. *Racing Post, 26 May 2006*

NORMAL

'Mick, if you want to do this job you've got to realise you are not a normal person' ... Irish champion jockey Johnny Murtagh to jump jockey Mick Fitzgerald.

NOTHING

'Nothing!' ... now retired jump jockey Luke Harvey, asked 'What do you miss most about your riding days?' *Racing Ahead magazine, July 2005*

'I tell you what I will say, I have nothing to say' ... Sir Michael Stoute was outraged when his appeal against a record £6,500 fine – his first – under the 'non-triers' rules over the running and riding of his Florimund at Windsor on 24 July 2006 was not only unsuccessful, but the fine was increased by £2,000. *The Sportsman, 5 August 2006*

NO WAITING

'I want my horses to continue racing until they are 12 or 13. I'm not prepared to rush them but owners are not prepared to wait.

I'm afraid I won't stand for any messing about' ... 60-year-old trainer Bob Jones explains why – perhaps he had only three horses in his charge on 30 July 2005.

NUDIST
'Nowhere on earth outside a nudist club is the dress code liable to be quite as fierce' ... writer William Hartston on Royal Ascot.

NUMBER
'To convince her, I told her to tell me her number, and if I could recite it after I raced, she'd have to let me take her out. I repeated it perfectly afterwards and we went for dinner at Pizza Express in Cambridge' ... old romantic Frankie Dettori on how he got his first date with the woman who would become his wife and mother to their five children, Catherine, who was 19 at the time. *You, 10 July 2005*

OF COURSE
'Until Great Leighs arrives, Taunton, which opened in 1927, remains Britain's newest racecourse. Frightening, really' ... David Ashforth. *Racing Post, 14 November 2005*

OFF HIS HEAD
'They went so fast early they took him off his head' ... jockey Ted Durcan on his mount Royal Millennium, who finished fourth in the valuable December 2004 Hong Kong Sprint.

OFFICIALS
'Too often I see horses in the parade ring who are patently way below their peak. Why can't officials see this, too?' ... former champion jump jockey Peter Scudamore. *Daily Mail, 29 December 2005*

OLDIES BUT GOLDIES
'It is not unusual to witness major races won by horses of my sort of age who are tubed, fired, gelded, visored, tongue-strapped and fitted with earplugs' ... Veteran racing fan Sir Clement Freud on visiting Garrison Savannah racecourse in Barbados. *Racing Post, 15 December 2004*

ON THE SLIDE
'Either you're womanising, or you're drinking too much, or you're gambling too much – somebody's always got a reason why you're on the slide' ... veteran trainer Michael Jarvis has a cynical take on life. *Racing Post, 27 May 2005*

ON YER BIKE
'I heard him yelling that it was a bike made for one, but I shouted for him to drive on. I was hanging off the back, clinging on to him for dear life, but he covered the last three miles at 100 miles an hour and drove me right to the weighing-room door. I made it with a minute to spare' ... Jamie Spencer on hijacking a passing motor cyclist when late en route to partner the favourite in the 6.10 at

Nottingham on Saturday, 20 August 2005. No happy ending, though – his mount, The Leather Wedge, finished third.

OPPORTUNITIES
'When I started punting they were called "races" not "betting opportunities"' ... Paul Haigh complains about the number of, er, races these days. *Racing Post, 29 July 2006*

OSTRACISED
'British racing is the best in the world. I get ostracised by my family for saying this because it's very un-Australian to accept that anything Britain does is superior. Bu there's an almost manic love of the horse here that you don't find in other countries, where betting is all that matters' ... departing Aussie chief executive of the BHB, Greg Nichols. *The Times, 30 June 2006*

OUT OF BODY EXPERIENCE
'When we were all standing in the winner's circle, I felt I was actually up in the air looking down on the whole thing' ... Arthur Hancock III, owner of 1982 Kentucky Derby winner, Gato Del Sol, on what he called 'the most intense moment of my life.'

OUT TO WIN
'You went out to win. Yes, I did cut up one or two, and them me. But you can't do two things, do your best to win all the time and be careful all the time' ... Lester Piggott interviewed in 2001 by the late Graham Rock.

OWNER

'I think if it had been Best Mate who had put his foot in that hole they would have coughed up. They just take us small owners for granted' ... Mike Disney is not overjoyed at his £500 – he claimed £964 – compensation from Leicester racecourse after his Two Tears fell on the flat when putting his foot in a hole caused by a collapsed drain.

'He said after the race that he had waited all his life to be told "This will win", and when it happened he had gone to pieces because of the weather' ... Trainer Bill O'Gorman, recalling the owner of easy winner Que Sera, who couldn't quite believe what he had been told.

'Martin (Pipe) came to me and said "Magnus is a horse I would like us to get", meaning I pay and he gets' ... owner David Johnson on the relationship between owners and trainers. *Racing Review, March 2002*

'Horses in England are now owned by people who don't even watch. They go to eat instead' ... Hong Kong-based trainer and German-based owner Ivan Allan. *Racing Review, December 2001*

'In the calendar there are no races confined to horses owned by owners whose horses have never won a race' ... interesting observation from Sir Clement Freud. *Racing Post, 17 May 2006*

'A lot of owners say "leave it to the trainer" but what does the trainer know that I don't?' ... an attitude which, probably, only an owner as wealthy and well established as Bill Gredley could get away with. *Sportsman, 29 May 2006.*

'I think she would have been quite happy for them to have been in the yard and never run' ... John Gosden, who used to train for 'caring' owner, Elizabeth Taylor. *Pacemaker, June 1999*

'Michael Owen doesn't go to bars, he doesn't get into fights; he owns racehorses and gambles to take his mind off things' ... Paul Merson, who self-confessedly took his gambling too far, supports Owen against critics of his hobby. *Daily Mail, 11 April 2006.*

PAC A MAC
'If Robin Bastiman were a piece of clothing, he would be a dark green pac-a-mac from Millets at £14.99' ... Peter Thomas on the Wetherby trainer. *Racing Post, 19 June 2006.*

PAGE THREE GIRL
'If she was human she'd be a model on page three of *The Times*, not *The Sun* – she's got class, you see' ... trainer Mark Rimell on his April 2005 Fontwell winner, Sun Pageant.

PAIN
'I find wearing tails and my father's top hat a pain in the arse' ... Charlie Brooks on going to Royal Ascot. *Daily Telegraph, 3 July 2006*

PAINT JOB

'A painter, mounted on a hydraulic lift, daubs the winning colours on a weather vane shaped like a horse and rider above the winner's circle in deference to a tradition dating back to 1909' ... Nicholas Godfrey at the 2005 Preakness Stakes run at Pimlico.

'This is racing's equivalent of Rembrandt being reduced to painting by numbers or Michelangelo producing a three-footed statue' ... Richard Edmondson pondering that Henry Cecil 'appears to be failing at the art of training racehorses'. *The Independent, 29 September 2005*

PALS?

'I find him quite a hard guy. You have to admire everything he's done in racing but he is hard to talk to. You can't get to know him – no one can. So you say "well done" but that's it. He's got a business to run and so have I – there's not a lot of time for pleasantries' ... Paul Nicholls on his great training rival, Martin Pipe, quoted by Donald McRae in *The Guardian, 18 April 2005*

PANTHEON

'I've seen dozens who were better. Dubai Millennium wouldn't even get to knock at the door of the thoroughbred pantheon, less still gain admittance' ... Tony Morris cannot believe Sheikh Muhammad's reported comment that his equine hero, Dubai Millennium was 'the best horse I have ever seen.' *Racing Post, 19 August 2005*

PANTOMIME

'The role as villains of racing's pantomime suits bookmakers down to the ground' ... oh no, it doesn't! Julian Muscat. *The Times, 30 August 2005*

PARADE

'While some of the public seem to enjoy them, I don't think any professionals enjoy the thought of a highly-strung horse using up energy that should be reserved for the race' ... trainer Michael Jarvis is not a fan of pre-race parades. *Sportsman, 21 September 2006*

PARA-MOTORING

'I've done sea-fishing, ornamental pheasants, golf, you name it – but I've finished up with the most dangerous one in the end' ... trainer Bryan McMahon reveal that he has taken up para-motoring – whatever that may be – to mark his spring 2005 retirement. *Racing Post, 30 March 2005*

PARTIES

'I'm not a great person for parties or prostituting myself. I'm not terribly good on my PR. I'm not in favour any more' ... Henry Cecil tries to justify his fall from the very top of his profession. He was certainly back in fashion in 2007. *The Independent, 29 September 2005*

PARTING IS SUCH SWEET ?

'The hardest part was ringing Stoutey (sic). He knew what was coming and told me he would have appreciated knowing far sooner. I didn't call because I wasn't sure what I was going to do' ... Kieren Fallon on telling Sir Michael Stoute that he was off to join the Coolmore team. *Sunday Times, 27 February 2005*

'It was an interdependent relationship. Kieren was always good on the horses' ... diplomatic reaction from Sir Michael. *Sunday Times, 27 February 2005*

'Kieren was said to have been disloyal to his former employer by quitting just a month ahead of the new season – but how many of us could be tempted from our present jobs if a better offer came along' ... 'Off The Bit' column in *Racing & Football Outlook* puts the story into its most basic context. March, 2005

PASSION

'If one that I have trained races against one that I have bred then I want the one that I have trained to win. Racing is my profession. Breeding is my passion' ... Luca Cumani. *Pacemaker, July 2006*

'Horses are my passion, and not just for racing – I am already breeding foals, and am seriously considering it as a career once my footballing days are over' ... England striker Michael Owen. *How To Spend It, June 2006*

'I have always had a passion for horse-racing' ... rugby
international Lawrence Dallaglio who became an owner because 'I
wanted to get a bit closer to it than just watching from the armchair'.
Evening Standard, 19 October 2006

PAST
**'The internet has made a complete horse's arse of on-course
betting. People like me will be a thing of the past one day'** ... Barry
Dennis predicts his own demise. *Guardian Weekend, 24 June 2006*

PEAS
**'They're grown from some seeds he found in the tomb. They're
about twice as big as ordinary peas'** ... Henry Cecil explains to Paul
Haigh that the sweet peas in his garden come from seeds found in
Tutankhamen's tomb which were passed to his stepfather, Cecil Boyd
Rochfort by his friend Howard Carter, who opened the historic vault.
Racing Post, 3 June 2007

PENALTY
**'If Ireland were in the World Cup and in a penalty shoot-out, the
man I would pick to take the fifth penalty would be Kieren'** ...
owner John Magnier on Fallon. *Racing Post, 3 July 2006*

'It was fantastic, although I still can't take a penalty' ... Darryl
Holland after being invited to recuperate from injury by training with
Glenn Roeder-managed Newcastle FC in August 2006.

PERSONAL AD
'Wanted: Romantic Male for L.T.R. Young looking and at heart 55yrs 'Mare' looking for her 'Motivator' to share fun and more in paddock' ... requested the advert listed under the heading 'Personal' in the *Racing Post* 'Classified Advertising' section of 3 December 2005. It asked for 'Pedigree Required – Love, passion, fun, respect, racing, travel, sun, excitement, happiness, good living' and explained 'My pedigree – blonde, sparkling blue eyes, well groomed, doesn't bite or kick! 5'9' medium healthy build. Needs honesty, love, cuddles.'

PERSPECTIVE
'Oh my god! How dreadful! If the plane had gone any further it would have ruined the track' ... Former editor of the *Irish Field*, Valentine Lamb, remembers a course commentator's remark at Cheltenham 'just before the first race in 1977,' when 'we witnessed a small plane skidding along and overturning after it crash-landed in a gale.' *Racing Post, 25 February 2005*

PET HATES
'Catering on racecourses has long been one of my pet hates. In the main it is overpriced and, in many cases, inedible' ... J A McGrath. *Daily Telegraph, March 2005*

PHILOSOPHICAL
'That's the National for you. No use kicking the cat. We live to fight another day' ... trainer Jonjo O'Neill's philosophical reaction as

Clan Royal, going so well in the 2005 National for Tony McCoy – neither of them had ever won the race – was carried out by loose horses. *Spectator, 16 April 2005*

'I'm delighted to have a horse. That's all that matters to me' ... trainer Jessica Harrington after her magnificent Moscow Flyer had failed to win for the first time when standing up over fences, at Punchestown on 26 April 2005.

PHOTO
'It's a photo ... a six thousand pounds photo, I might add' ... TV commentator and owner of one of the horses, Attivo, in the 1974 Chester Cup – Sir Peter O'Sullevan. His horse got the verdict.

'The starting of two year olds is like photography of a child; if it is not taken on the first smile, then the operation is a failure and each attempt after, worse' ... charming analogy during a time of unrest with the behaviour of Starters in Irish racing, by large-scale breeder William Pallin in October 1886.

PIGGOTT
'I have always thought that if Lester had ridden Shergar in every one of his races, he would never have been beaten' ... Michael Stoute. *Daily Telegraph, 1 June 2006*

PIPE DREAM
'I like to say I rode as many winners as Martin Pipe' ... trainer

David Baker, whose solitary success in the saddle came in a point-to-point at Whitton Castle. *The Times, 30 July 2005*

PIPE OPENER

'His desperate tactics in trying to hang on to "his" championship bordered on the unprofessional, unsporting, underhand and uncaring' … yes, it's the 'bordered' which is significant as owner David Jackson, on the Paul Nicholls side of the race to become champion jumps trainer, berates Martin Pipe on the other. *Racing Post, 1 May 2005*

PISSED

'There were a few incidents. Like getting drunk with my mates when I should have been taking Rachel Stevens out on a date, and attending the last audition for (reality TV show) The Farm when still pissed from the night before, which made me stop and think about what I was doing to myself' … reformed hell-raising jockey Martin Cotton, quoted by Graham Green in the *Racing Post* of 8 June 2005, won the date via a Radio 1 competition.

PISSED OFF

'The horse was back from a workout, and I had to go to the ladies' room. I sat down, and I realised that all the mikes were running. I had to get back up and pull all the mikes off. I was relieved that I didn't pee for the entire world' … US trainer Jennie Sahadi on being wired for sound by TV stations prior to the 2000 Kentucky Derby.

'I think that if I were a girl, I'd be a little pissed off about it – I'd want to be riding against the men on equal terms' … trainer and former jockey David Nicholls, whose wife Alex Greaves was one of the top female riders of her generation, is against a suggestion to allow women riders a gender allowance. *Racing Post, 24 July 2005*

'Just piss off!' … Having just seen his hot St Leger favourite Meadow Court beaten in the 1965 race, the last thing crooner Bing Crosby wanted to address was a request for an autograph from a keen fan. *Pacemaker's* Tony Morris, who was there reporting on the race, recalled Bing's rebuff. *Pacemaker, September 2005*

PIZZLING DOWN

'Goodwood has "pizzle", a combination of pissing rain and mizzle, that drifts in from the sea and refuses to go away until the day's racing has been abandoned' … Peter Thomas on Goodwood's abandoned meeting of May 2005 – mizzle being a Cornish combination of mist and drizzle.

PLANE TRICKY

'He's just like an aeroplane. The trouble with this plane is that he hijacks himself' … Paul Carberry's take on Harchibald, his 2005 Champion Hurdle ride on whom proved the most controversial of the Festival, probably the year, possibly the decade.

PLUMBING THE DEPTHS

'I've always regarded having a jockey as a bit like having a

plumber. **What matters is the hot water coming out of the right tap. If you like your plumber, then so much the better'** ... Sir Mark Prescott. *Pacemaker, July 2005*

POINTLESS
'I don't see the point of riding a horse with no chance of winning. That's just asking for trouble' ... fortunately for him Mick Fitzgerald had reached a level of seniority in the game to afford to take this stance when he told Andrew Longmore of his strategy. *Sunday Times, 13 February 2005*

POKER PUNTERS
'It is imperative that the card club blends into the racing operation to grow both businesses' ... Randall Simpson of Canterbury Park racecourse in Minnesota where the introduction of poker playing facilities to the track has been rewarded by the poker players accounting for 'some five percent of all handle' at the course, whereas people playing slot machines at the tracks gamble virtually nothing on the horses. *Racing Post, 23 December 2005*

POLAR BEARS
'The Guineas are too early – I found two dead polar bears on our gallops this week, and a penguin nicked my scarf' ... Mick Channon in March 2006.

POLITIC OR NOT?
'I still cannot shake off the sense that there is something rather

improper in betting on an election result.' ... former Foreign Secretary and keen racing man, Robin Cook. *Racing Post, 23 February 2005.*

'The first time I met him was at the second-last at Chepstow on Welsh Grand National day some 20 years ago. You don't go there unless you really love the game' ... Brough Scott reacts to the news on 6 August 2005 of the death of Robin Cook, adding 'no politician as senior as him has been such a true racing fan for 100 years.'

PONY
'When I was 12 I was cycling past our neighbours, going to a hurling game, and there was a pony tied to the gate. For some reason I jumped on him and from then on that's all I wanted to do' ... how Paddy Brennan became a jockey. *The Times, 16 April 2005*

POOR
'The billionaire Bill Gates could embark on a day's racing at Goodwood and return a poor man' ... Peter Oborne. *Evening Standard, 31 July 2006*

POP CONCERT
'The great majority were young, more the sort of age group that you would expect to see at a pop concert in Britain rather than on a racecourse. Many were decked out with scarves and shirts in the Deep Impact colours' ... Greg Wood of *The Guardian* on the youth of the thousands of Japanese who trekked to Paris to see their equine

hero, Deep Impact finish 3rd in the 2006 Arc. *The Guardian, 2 October, 2006*

PORCELAIN
'If you are lucky enough to have fine porcelain on your table then it really is a pleasure to sit down to eat' ... French trainer Robert Collet explaining how he rarely goes racing now, except when he has top runners in action. *Pacemaker, October 2005*

PORK PIE
'A bookmaker once told me that if you see a man on a race track with a pork pie in one hand and a Mars bar in the other, you can bet your life he has just backed a loser in the last race' ... no, I'm not sure either, what pro punter Dave Nevison was on about in his *Racing & Football Outlook* column of 2-8 May, 2006

PORN
'Anyone would think we were talking about letting internet porn sites stage nude community singing on the bandstand after racing' ... Peter Thomas cannot understand why Royal Ascot will not permit sponsorship of its races. *Racing Post, 20 October 2005*

POSITIVE
'No shouting. Patience please. Positive thoughts only. Leave other mental shortcomings outside' ... Notice on display in Somerset trainer Nathan Rossiter's yard in 2005.

POST
'Be cautious and go not too soon, the post is the place to win at'
... timeless advice from top jump jockey of his day, Tom Olliver,
written shortly before the Grand National – a race he won three times
– in 1869.

POST IT NOTE
**'When Richard (Quinn) stands next to it, it'll be reminiscent of a
scene from Jack and The Beanstalk'** ... Kempton PR man Johnno
Spence on the 8ft tall winning post from the track acquired by jockey
Quinn – whose first winner was there in 1981 – in May 2005 after
they staged their final Flat meeting on turf before the diggers moved
in to turn it all-weather.

PRAYER
**'The last resorts of a clerk of the course are private prayer and
humble pie'** ... Kirkland Tellwright who holds that post at Haydock
on the problems with producing the right going and the right going
description. *Racing Post, 13 August 2006*

PREMATURE
'Premature ejockulation' ... Clare Balding's graphic description of an
unseated jockey – male, no doubt. *Daily Mail, 13 April 2007*

PRESSING MATTER
'Chepstow – racing's answer to the Black Hole of Calcutta' ...
racing writer Geoff Lester is unimpressed with Chepstow's facilities
for hacks. *13 December 2004*

PRESS UPS
'Doing six press-ups is standard procedure to pass the doctor after breaking a collarbone and I have never done them before' ... Frankie Dettori, who returned from a lengthy lay off at Newmarket on 26 August 2005

PRESSURE
'Jockeys should always be under pressure' ... Martin Pipe, December 2004.

'The pressure on the Leger has been growing for years as the racing and breeding industries changed around it, and there is only so much stress that any structure can take, no matter how deep its foundations' ... Greg Wood is not optimistic about the future of the oldest Classic, concluding, 'Racing and breeding have moved on and the Leger has been left behind.' *Guardian, 4 September 2006.*

'I do not feel under pressure riding the favourite in a big race. I'd rather have it and lose than not have it. I am not afraid to lose. If you are, you have already lost' ... Mick Fitzgerald. *The Times, 21 September 2006.*

'I don't do pressure. Pressure is for tyres and footballs' ... Irish trainer Jim Bolger, reported by Brough Scott. *Sunday Telegraph, 15 October 2006*

PRICES

'There are some major games being played with the prices of horses these days, and the risk of getting your fingers burnt if you get sucked in is higher than ever' ... pro punter Dave Nevison with a warning to the unwary. *Racing & Football Outlook, 30 May-5 June 2006*

PRINCIPLE

'I get irritated by Channel 4 because of the intrusive manner of their presentation, and on a point of principle I won't speak to them' ... David Elsworth. *Pacemaker, April 2006.*

PRIVILEGE

'A month ago I went to the last fence between Tony McCoy and Ruby Walsh, the very best in the game. That's a privilege no other sport can give' ... and amateur rider Captain Lucy Horner, 27, the first female platoon commander in the British infantry, is no mean performer herself, finishing second on Joint Authority, described in a formbook as 'lunatic front-runner professionals can do nothing with', in Sandown's Royal Artillery Gold Cup in February 2005.

'Imagine if you had privileges and didn't make use of them' ... amateur jockey David Dunsdon – 'I found it quite hard' – who wrestled with how to come to terms with his father paying £240,000 for a horse, Joly Bey, so that he could ride it in the National. *Sunday Times, 3 April 2005*

PRIZE MONEY

'The prize-money might not be great, but where would you rather run your horse – Southwell and Wolverhampton, or somewhere like this' ... trainer David Evans with a vote for scenic Les Landes on Jersey. *Racing Post, 10 September 2006*

PROPER MAN

'Hughes walked in through the crowd with his young rider. He's a proper man.' ... Charlie Brooks on the protective way in which trainer Dessie Hughes supported rookie jockey Roger Loughran who had mistaken the winning post and begun celebrating too early on Hi Cloy at Leopardstown and been beaten in December 2005. Tony McCoy later said he went to sympathise, but 'the poor chap just couldn't speak.'

PROSTITUTES

'The business of training racehorses has gone the same way as prostitutes. Too many amateurs about' ... comment of the late Sir Noel Murless, reported in 1996 by daughter Julie Cecil.

PUB

'I ride the horse out and he either gallops by himself or with my dog. There have been occasions when I've been to the pub on him' ... George Wareham reveals the training secrets of his only horse, 14 year old The Newsman who won at Plumpton in April 2006.

PUNCH

'This guy, a local, actually punched me as I was weighing in and no one did anything about it' ... 25-year-old Charlotte Kerton, the first woman to win in Bahrain explains the reaction of a local jockey after she rode a double there. *Racing Post, 23 April 2006*

PUNDITRY

'As far as punditry goes, I always say after a meeting, "Got away with it again, I think"' ... Willie Carson. *Daily Telegraph, 29 July 2006*

PUNTERS

'Never mind those hunched over computer screens in darkened rooms, the vast majority of punters crave a slice of free cash paid in person by the betting shop clerk' ... Julian Muscat. *The Times, 30 August 2005*

PUSSYCATS

'All these good horses over here are pussycats; they only have to sneeze and they're off to stud' ... Aussie owner Paul Makin, who tried unsuccessfully to arrange a match race after his Starcraft had beaten Dubawi, ridden by a criticised Frankie Dettori, in the QEII Stakes at Newbury. *Racing Post, 28 September 2005*

PUT AWAY

'Did he really have to put readers away in such a fashion?' ... *Racing Post's* James Pyman contrasts trainer Richard Fahey's pre-Ayr Gold Cup comment that 'he's been disappointing on his two last runs and I don't know why' with his comments after Fonthill Road won the race; 'put this one down to John Patterson and add genius to the end of his name' when explaining that the equine back specialist had transformed his horse before his 16/1 triumph. *Racing Post, 17 September 2006*

PYRAMID

'If Sea Bird had run in this year's Derby he would probably have finished tenth. It's obvious. We are breeding more horses than fifty years ago, so there is a bigger base to the pyramid, and therefore the top of the pyramid has to be higher than it would for a smaller based pyramid. It's logical' ... Luca Cumani. *Pacemaker, July 2006*

QUAINT

'Some see being kept in the dark as one of the quaint quirks of the British turf, while others see it for what it is – a denial of useful information for which there is no worthy excuse' ... 'Newsboy' of the *Daily Mirror* complaining at the lack of info about horses' racing weights in this country. *Daily Mirror, 27 May 2006*

QUALITY

'Crowds are dwindling and the fault lies with a glut of moderate racing. It's screaming at you that people want quality not quantity' ... Barry Dennis. *The Sun, 17 September 2005*

QUE?

'The French don't win our greatest race – simple as that and we

should take great delight when Visindar is stuffed. His trainer (Andre Fabre) thinks he's Napoleon and is the most sullen man on the planet' ... controversial bookie/columnist Barry Dennis rubbishing the chances of 2006 Derby favourite Visindar, duly well beaten. But who did Dennis fancy? 'Step forward Frankie Dettori and Linda's Lad' declared Dennis – perhaps overlooking the fact that Linda's Lad was trained in, er, France .. by, er, Andre Fabre. And no, he didn't win, either! *The Sun, 3 June 2006*

QUICKER

'It is reckoned quicker for a horse to get from Lambourn to Belmont (New York) than it is to Ayr' ... James Willoughby on the ease of international travel – or the difficulty of domestic travel, perhaps. *Pacemaker, October 2005*

RACECOURSE

'In the pre-parade ring Orpen Wide slipped and fell on the slick, damp tarmac – which a track that cares for horses would have replaced with a rubberoid surface or at least covered with sawdust.' ... an unappreciative owner, Sir Clement Freud, berates Windsor. *Racing Post, 27 April 2005*

'I often think of Leicester as the Longchamp of the Midlands' ... the only one who does, then. Robert Cooper in *The Sportsman, 3 October 2006*

RACEGOER
'Osama liked horseracing. But when they started playing music at the racecourse he would get up and walk out, because he thought music was haram (forbidden by Islam)' ... Issam el-Turabi, former business associate of Osama Bin Laden. *Guardian, December 2004*

RACE FIXING
'There is a strong likelihood that during such a period, racing would be severely damaged by the possibility of further race-fixing and the perception of such, and by the adverse reaction of many members of the racing public to the concept that a jockey charged with an offence which is so close to the heart of the sport is permitted to continue to participate' ... Former High Court judge Sir Michael O'Connell who chaired the Horseracing Regulatory Authority which took the decision to suspend jockeys Kieren Fallon, Fergal Lynch and Darren Williams until their trial for fraud could take place. *Racing Post, 8 July 2006*

'Whether the defendants, as we must now get used to calling them, are found guilty or innocent probably won't make much difference to the betting public. The betting public's too cynical to care' ... Paul Haigh. *Racing Post, 8 July 2006*

'Guantanamo Bay rules now apply in British racing' ... Rolf Johnson, 'The Scout', of the *Daily Express*, is not impressed with the suspension of the accused jockeys.

'Can racing afford to have newcomers asking 'Isn't that the jockey who was arrested? How come he's still riding?'' ... Julian Wilson looks from a different direction at the problem. *Racing Post, 11 July 2006*

RACES!

'Races! A congregation of all the worst blackguards in the county, mixed with the greatest fools!' ... The Duke of Omnium in Athony Trollope's *The Duke's Children*, written in 1880. plus ça change

RACETRACKS

'Twenty four of them on the back of a big, flatbed lorry. Every time they went over a bump they lost a couple. They toured the racetracks of England – Kempton, Ascot, Epsom. Dad always had a harmonica in his inside pocket' ... Rolling Stone, Ronnie Wood, reminisces about his Dad's harmonica band. *Mojo, April 2007*

RACEY

'I had watched Quinn play for Newcastle so I offered him double or quits for a race over half a furlong. Blow me, he went so far clear he turned round and ran backwards, laughing at me' ... ace bookie/sprinter Barry Dennis regretted trying to get back the fifty quid he'd just lost to former footballer turned trainer, Micky 'Sumo' Quinn at Windsor on 13 June 2005.

RACING

'While the English are fond of their racing the Irish can't live

without it' ... American author, Bill Barich, in his 2005 book, *A Fine Place to Daydream*.

'Domestically the sport appears increasingly divisive, blinkered and threatened by public apathy' ... Julian Wilson on racing, not in Britain but in South Africa. *Racing Post, 10 March 2005*

'I've had very good afternoons of friendship with people I've never met before and never met afterwards, but for those three hours we were united in our love for horse racing' ... Robin Cook on the delights of a day at the races. *The Festival, March 2005*

'Racing was at the front of the queue when reactionaries were handed out' ... Lydia Hislop. *The Times, 23 March 2005*

'If you take me out of racing there's not much that I fit into' ... apart from martial arts, that is. Karate black-belt jockey Alan Munro, who admits getting into the sport as a result of a John Craven's Newsround TV feature on Steve Cauthen which 'made the whole idea of being a jockey very glamorous'. *Racing Post, 25 March 2005*

'It is the tension between honesty and dodginess, both in men and horses that gives it much of its charm' ... writer Terence Blacker on horse racing. *The Independent, 18 March 2005*

'Racing people are an inexplicable mix of hard money and soft centres' ... Alastair Down. *Racing Post, 17 March 2005*

Just like dram drinking; momentary excitement and wretched intervals; full consciousness of the mischievous effects of the habit and equal difficulty in abstaining from it' ... owner, gambler and steward Charles Greville's opinion in 1838 of, allegedly, racing – some suspected he really meant betting, a vice at which he excelled. In 1851 he reportedly won £14,000 on the result of a single race.

'The racing world is stuffed with lunatics, criminals, idiots, charmers, bastards and exceptionally nice people' ... racing writer, the late Jeffrey Bernard in 1987.

REALIST
'As I turned away, I thought there might be something in that' ... Barry Geraghty remembers being abused by a racegoer at Listowel who told him: 'You'd be nothing without Moscow Flyer'. *The Guardian, 14 March 2005.*

'I am an optimist, but I'm also a realist. You tend to be once you've broken your neck' ... Mick Fitzgerald in conversation with the *Guardian*'s Donald McRae. He broke his neck but it was misdiagnosed and when that was corrected, added Fitzgerald, who had been in great pain, 'I was actually quite relived it was quite serious – I'd been worried I was getting soft.' *Guardian, 20 December 2005*

RECORD BREAKER
'I understand it's a vain act, but one I'll be proud of' ... not

surprisingly, handler Steve Asmussen, was pleased to become the first US trainer there to send out 500 winners in a season when Smooth Bid won at Remington Park, Oklahoma in November 2004.

RECREATION
'Were gentlemen to remember that racing is a recreation and were they to speculate less deeply, they would set a better example' ... *The Times, 4 June 1874*

REFUSING TO LISTEN
'Pull up your horse now' ... was the bizarre announcement over the tannoy system by a steward at the Braes of Derwent Point-to-Point meeting on 16 April 1994, directed at Austrian rider, Hans Waltl, who carried on trying to complete the course after his horse Simon refused twice at the second, then again at the third, fourth and eighth fences before being lapped by the rest of the runners.

RELATIONSHIP
'We don't live together. She actually lives quite a long way away – and it works out really well because it's impossible to live a normal life with me' ... divorced once, trainer Paul Nicholls on his long-distance relationship. *The Guardian, 18 April 2005*

'Relationships come a very distant second to racing' ... jockey Mick Fitzgerald. *The Guardian, 20 December 2005.*

RELATIVE

'I can never understand why people get so excited when J P McManus has a hundred grand or whatever on something, because it's just small change to him. All betting is relative' ... Alastair Down. *Sports Adviser, 24 January 2002*

RESPITE

'Racing and breeding are almost certainly the subjects which our sovereign knows more about than any others, a deserved respite from dull official duties. I suspect she would have made an excellent trainer' ... Geoffrey Wheatcroft – crawler!. *The Spectator, 24 June 2006*

RESTLESS

'If I go to bed knowing that one of my horses is racing the next day, I will be staring at the alarm clock at 3am and probably 4 and 5 as well. It will be a horrible, restless night' ... England striker Michael Owen. *The Times, 16 January 2006.*

RESTRICTION

'How odd that there is a restriction in England that restricts the ownership listing of a horse to 40 characters If you are a partner in a horse, much of the enjoyment is in seeing your name underneath your horse in the racecard This may seem unimportant to many, but how puerile and absurd is a restriction like this? There can surely be no legitimate reason why a 10 member partnership cannot have all the names of the owners listed' ...

Pacemaker editor Darryl Sherer gets hot under the collar, and should win the support of the 230 or so owners of Derby winner, Motivator. July 2005

RETICENCE
'There was a reticence to commit to a return visit. It had been a brilliant day in a beautiful part of the countryside, but next time another brave horse might die, and they didn't want to be there to witness that' ... John Inverdale, a racing fan, reflects on a trip to Plumpton with novice racegoers shaken by the near-death experience of a fallen runner. *Daily Telegraph, 19 April 2006*

RETIREMENT
'I came in on a winner and now I am going out on one' ... Graham McCourt, whose first ride in 1975 had been a winner, bowed out after winning on Sister Stephanie at Chepstow on 27 March 1996.

'The day it doesn't affect me is the day I will pack up' ... trainer Alan King on racecourse fatalities. *The Times, 18 December 2004*

'He took a week and went up to the mountains on sabbatical and just said the Lord has told him to move on and minister back here to help the Race Track Chaplaincy of America' ... Pat Day's agent Doc Danner on the top US rider's July 2005 decision to retire.

'I went outside, turned the sauna off, put the kettle on and made myself a mug full of tea, got the scales and threw them into the

field, and I rang Michael Chapman and Neville Bycroft and told them I wouldn't be riding that day or any other day' ... Dandy Nicholls on the day he decided to quit the saddle. *Racing Post, 12 August 2005*

'There is a piece of my heart that would love to continue riding, but my body can't take it any more.' ... US jockey Gary Stevens explains his November 2005 retirement after 26 successful years in the saddle.

'Though I will miss the thrill of physical competition I have been accustomed to for the past 31 years, this new seat will be far less dangerous than my old one. And it also includes lunch' ... ace US jockey Jerry Bailey, 48, quitting the saddle to go into TV in January 2006.

'Swan, you should have retired yesterday' .... Charlie Swan, having announced in April 2003 that he would be retiring, fell at the last on his penultimate ride, receiving the wry comment from a punter on his way back in.

RETIRING
'I've always struggled with my weight. I rode nine lots of work the other day in a sweatsuit, then got on the treadmill, had a swim – and lost half a pound' ... 36-year-old galloping granny, pioneering girl jockey Alex Greaves, announced her retirement from the saddle in March 2005. 'Being a girl in this game you have to work twice as hard to prove yourself,' she said.

'**Whenever I've had a fall lately I have been left feeling dazed, which I didn't in the old days. As much as I love riding I have to put my health before my career**' ... short but eloquent explanation by 31-year-old Irishman, Jim Culloty, who won three Cheltenham Gold Cups on Best Mate, announcing his retirement on 19 July 2005. His weighing room colleague Carl Llewellyn observed: 'He's married to a girl with a lot of money, so he might as well go and enjoy it.'

'**I'll still be on the gallops every day. I can pick the dog shite (sic) up**' ... Ginger McCain tells Lydia Hislop of his plans for impending retirement. *The Times, 17 October 2005*

RETREAT
'**You can live in a safe cocoon or you can give yourself a kick up the backside and take on a challenge. You don't win battles if you start to retreat**' ... David Elsworth explains why he quit Whitsbury for Newmarket after 25 years. *Pacemaker, April 2006*

REVVING UP
'**I always say I am visiting my Gloucester diocese**' ... Canon Michael Hunter, rector of Grimsby's euphemism for his annual visit to the Cheltenham Festival, as told to *The Sun's* Claude Duval in February 2005.

RHYTHM
'**Good horses must have rhythm**' ... Sir Michael Stoute. *Daily Telegraph, 22 June 2006*

RISK

'Many devotees of National Hunt anxiously suspect there may be room for improvement in the measures meant to ensure the safety of horses at the jumping game's supreme event. They recognise substantial risk is intrinsic to the sport and that they will always have huge difficulty in balancing thrills with an acceptable degree of hazard' ... Hugh McIlvanney over the debate on the fatalities at the 2006 Cheltenham Festival. *Sunday Times, 19 March 2006*

ROBBERY

'I was once in a bookies that was actually being robbed and there were still punters trying to get their 10p combination forecasts on at Monmore' ... cynical punter N Swann of Edinburgh wrote to tell *Racing & Football Outlook* of his bizarre betting shop experience in March 2005.

'Punters in the UK and Ireland have left behind the best part of £50m today – as much as the Securitas robbery, only ours is legal' ... William Hill PR man, David Hood celebrates a profitable Wednesday at the 2006 Cheltenham Festival.

ROGUES

'I do not say that all those who go racing are rogues and vagabonds, but I do say that all the rogues and vagabonds seem to go racing' ... true today, too, as it was when top South African owner Sir Abe Bailey (1864-1940), who had moved to England, said it after winning the Gimcrack Stakes at York in 1925 with Lex.

ROYAL APPROVAL

'I've got two things to announce to you of the greatest importance. The first is that the Grand National was won by Hedgehunter. The second is to say to you that despite Becher's Brook and The Chair and all kinds of other terrible obstacles, my son has come through and I'm very proud and wish them well' ... The Queen, quoted by guest at the Charles-Camilla wedding reception, Stephen Fry on 9 April 2005.

'I am happiest when I have no public engagements to fulfil. When I can smoke a really good cigar and read (must I confess it?) a really good novel on the quiet. When I can, like plain Mr Jones, go to a race-meeting without it being chronicled in the papers next day that "His Royal Highness the Prince of Wales has taken to gambling very seriously, and yesterday lost more money than ever he can afford to pay"' ... King Edward VII's entry into his daughter's, the Duchess of Fife, Confessional Album.

'Come on Prinny, make a name for yourself' ... Sheikh Mohammed's wife, Princess Haya recalls a comment from the crowd whilst she contested a lady amateur's race at Killarney which she dubbed her favourite moment in racing. *Irish Field, October 2006*

ROYAL ASCOT

'To me, Royal Ascot, wherever it is, is a garden party for birds in tiny frocks and big hats' ... bookie Barry Dennis. *The Sun, 18 June 2005*

'The Monaco Grand Prix at Bournemouth or Cowes Week at Hull'
… *Daily Mail* disparages Royal Ascot at York

'Royal Ascot would be just another racing "festival" were it not for the 12,000 who attend in top hats and tails and who, along with the Queen, give the meeting its sense of occasion, tradition and pageantry, things all too readily air-brushed out of modern life' …
Marcus Armytage. *Daily Telegraph, 16 June 2005*

'The muted reception given to the winners at last year's Royal Ascot spoke at best of indifference, at worst of arrogance. A switch of venue, albeit temporary might restore a proper sense of theatre to the greatest festival of racing in the world' … Andrew Longmore. *Sunday Times, 12 June 2005*

'The Northern girls' chests were wonderful and the singongs at the end of the day's racing were truly emotional' … John McCririck on Royal Ascot at York. *Evening Standard, September 2005.*

'The picnic scene was just not up to scratch. I felt it was a bit like the Americans trying to Troop the Colour' … banker David Murray-Wood on entertaining clients at the Royal Ascot at York meeting. *Evening Standard, September 2005.*

RUDE GIRL
'Jenny Pitman trained two winners of the Grand National. She is

also, and by a considerable margin, the rudest woman I have ever met' … Simon Barnes. *The Times, 9 April 2005*

RUMOUR
'I've heard the rumour – it's bollocks, and please put that in the paper. If it's true, I'll pull my trousers down in the front window of Selfridges. I'm going to die in the job of taking on Coral, Ladbrokes and Hills' … Fred Done denies that he is to sell his shops to one of the 'big three'. *Racing Post, 12 February 2006*

RUSH
'The easiest way to stop a horse and to escape detection by civilian spectators is probably to rush him off his feet' … trainer Bill O'Gorman. *Pacemaker, March 2007*

RUSSIAN AROUND
'The racecourse is vast – bigger than Belmont Park. They have very grand ideas, one of which is to put on six $1 million races at a festival to rival the Breeders' Cup' … trainer Paul Cole on ambitious plans for Russia's first international racecourse Kazan, 700 miles east of Moscow, in Tatarstan, which opened on 27 August 2005.

SACRIFICE
'All my life I have been trying for this, and for what have I sacrificed it?' … distraught MP, Lord George Bentinck, who sold his horse Surplice to finance his political career, only for the beast to win the 1848 Derby.

SAD

'I go home to Southwell and stay with my Mum. I can chill out a bit and go to bed early – that's quite sad for a 23 year old, isn't it?' ... up and coming jockey Hayley Turner. *The Times, 6 January 2006*

'I'm very sad to say, for the foreseeable future, it's goodbye from Goodwood' ... after a 50-year association between the BBC and the glorious racecourse, Clare Balding signs off for probably the last time on 27 August 2006.

SADDLING UP

'Lying in hospital gives you the time to analyse whether you really want this any more, and all I could think of was getting back in the saddle' ... Mick Fitzgerald far from down despite discovering that rather than a routine injury he had actually suffered a broken neck, in August 2005. He would later hint at retirement, only to carry on.

SAMURAI

'The samurai philosophy is that when you struggle you must do so gracefully. Your exterior must be very cold, even if your interior is very hot. I try to be like that. I think he has the spirit of samurai too' ... Japanese equine superstar Deep Impact's trainer Yasuo Ikee on himself and the horse. *Racing Post 12 September 2006*

SANDWICHES

'We usually get together on a Friday, sit in the parking lot and eat sandwiches while we look over the races. Brian is the racing guy. I

just throw around names I like. Eventually he gives in and we go
with the names I like' ... which is just as well for Brian Wien, 45,
from New Jersey and his pal of 25 years standing, Tom Ritchie, 55 –
by this method they laid out $192 on a combination bet involving
four horses in an effort to win the 2005 Kentucky Derby superfecta.
So when they (he!) came up with Giacomo, Closing Argument, Afleet
Alex and Don't Get Mad in that order they collected a cool
$864,253.50.

SANDY, SURE!
'I'm a bit like Rommel in that I've got a lot of followers on the
sand and when they see a bit of money for one of mine they tend
to step out' ... maverick trainer Barney Curley after his Le Soleil
landed a hefty gamble at Wolverhampton in late September 2005.

SAPS
'Am I alone in having run out of sympathy for those saps who lose
their life savings to betting scams run by the unscrupulous to
fleece the gullible?' ... asked Peter Thomas in the *Post* on 1 August
2005. No.

SATANIC
'I don't think the name is so much satanic as spiritual. We're
delving into the beyond, not down to the devil' ... interesting
defence of Ouija Board's name by owner, Lord Derby to Sue Mott.
Daily Telegraph, 2 June 2007

SAUNA
'Many of my colleagues live on chips, pies, crisps and lager. If they changed their diet and lifestyle, perhaps they could quit the sauna' ... Dale Gibson is not convinced by calls to raise the minimum weight carried by fellow jockeys. *Racing Post, 14 February 2006*

SCAB
'I'd hate to think of our racing going like American racing – that's like watching a scab form' ... Mick Channon. *Daily Telegraph, 14 April 2006*

SCANT
'The truth is that historically, with some welcome and popular exceptions, Flat jockeys have shown by their actions that they have scant regard for the public' ... a comment by Alistair Down that jockeys were not over-impressed with, in the wake of their lack of support for stewards inquiries to be held in public. *Racing Post, 23 August 2005*

SCARED
'I was truly scared – I had no idea how traumatic even a normal birth is' ... A man who has suffered multiple injuries in his profession as a jockey, Mick Fitzgerald, couldn't cope with watching his girlfriend Chloe Jackman deliver their son Zac, who weighed in at 10lbs in August 2006.

SCHOOLING

'A racecourse is a place for racing. It is not for schooling or for trying to get a handicap mark' ... John Bridgeman, chairman of the Horseracing Regulatory Authority indicating that he is keen to change certain attitudes in the sport, *The Sportsman* 8 August 2006. Compare and contrast with Bill O'Gorman's take in *Pacemaker*, August 2006: 'Any initiatives to eliminate our non-triers will struggle to succeed in the present atmosphere which effectively encourages non-triers.'

SCIENCE

'We don't normally engage with scientists, but we have heard from scientists and have received a number of theories on how to prevent this problem' ... clerk of the course Edward Gillespie, revealing that Cheltenham were looking for scientific help to deal with the recurring problem of low sun blinding jockeys as they jump fences in the straight. *Racing Post, 27 November 2005*

SCOUNDRELS

'It is unfortunate that the noble and useful sport of horse racing cannot exist and be enjoyed without giving birth to, as a class, the most unmitigated scoundrels that are to be found in the world. The fraudulent 'list-keeper' (betting shop operator), and the welcher of all grades and degrees, represent a seething mass of cunning, audacity, roguery, and crime that is to be found in connection with no other national amusement except horse-racing' ... some things never change, eh? *Dublin University Magazine, May 1874*

SCREAMING

'Luca (Cumani) – he's one of the best trainers in the country, but his horse has just won and he can stand there all articulate and tell you this and tell you that. Me, I'll be screaming me 'ead off' ... Dandy Nicholls. *Racing Post, 12 August 2005*

SEASIDE

'Maureen and I have worked hard to get where we are and we're not going to throw it away for a dull future in a seaside bungalow. I'll consider cutting the number of horses when I'm 100 and not before' ... 72 year old trainer Clive Brittain in no hurry to retire. *Takesport, 15 September 2006*

SEASON

'Summer has never been my time of year. Wrong sort of racing and a lack of proper winter sports are to blame' ... John Francome *Racing Ahead, October 2005*

SECOND

'Finishing second in a horse race is the worst feeling in the world. Bar none' ... Tony McCoy. *Daily Telegraph, 25 May 2006*

SECRECY

'British racing is built on handicapping and therefore secrecy. It's no surprise, although rather disheartening, to find even the greenest apprentice seems to have been told only to talk on a need-to-know basis' ... Lydia Hislop bemoans an apparent unwillingness to confide in the media. *The Times, 24 August 2005*

'There is an outdated culture of secrecy about even the most routine details that would be amusing if it wasn't so insulting to the public, whose betting keeps the more successful trainers in expensive German motor cars' ... Alastair Down on trainers. *Racing Post, 4 December 2005*

SECRET
'On one occasion in Moscow the results pages of the *Racing Post* were faxed through to the ambassador's residence and served up on my breakfast tray with SECRET stamped on every page' ... the late former Foreign Secretary and racing fan, Robin Cook.

SELF CONFIDENCE
'The thousands of winners, bucket loads of awards, mountains of newspaper clippings extolling his virtues as a jockey have not given him an ounce of confidence in his own ability' ... Clare Balding on A P McCoy. *The Observer, 5 December 2004*

SENSITIVE
'In England, Dettori would have been stood down for the rest of the season. In France, they are less sensitive about horseflesh. They eat it, after all' ... writer Pete Nichols on Lammtarra's 1995 Arc win in which 'Dettori hit the colt 16 times in the final three furlongs.'

SEX
'I've planned a day of group sex for myself and twenty of my

closest of friends – all of whom are women' ... Claude Duval
reporting on what John Francome allegedly planned for his 52nd
birthday celebration on 13 December 2004. *The Sun, 11
December 2004*

**'They dig the hole for her to put her back legs in so Star Way can
reach'** ... Tim Bodle, owner of 1988 Melbourne Cup winner Empire
Rose, a lofty 17.1 hands high and weighing a massive 650 kgs,
explains why Windsor Stud attendants dig a 30 centimetre hole in
the serving barn floor when her paramour, Star Way, arrives to
service her. *Racetrack, November 1995*

SEXISM
'Its win or bust. The jockey could win with a double handful' ...
Thommo on *Talksport*, discussing the chances of Hayley Turner on
her Redcar ride, Wunderbra, to which show host Mike Parry
quipped, 'The horse has his knockers'. Hayley just went about her
business, winning on the 5/2 shot.

**'Sexism isn't a factor in Canada. People don't look at me as a
female rider, and I'm as hard and strong as anyone else in the
weighing room'** ... 24 year old Canadian champion apprentice,
English-born Emma-Jayne Wilson, after chalking up over 250
winners in that country where apprentices are usually known as
'bugs' but the media dubbed Emma-Jayne as 'Shebiscuit'.

SEXY STUFF
'In racing papers and on tip sheets you get phone numbers for

shops that sell sex aids, orgasm stimulants, sadomasochist software – surely that should be hardware – and I found a special offer for a pill that takes five minutes to induce an erection which lasts an hour' … Sir Clement Freud is a little surprised at what he found whilst visiting Florida in February 2005. *Racing Post, 2 March 2005*

'I don't know. I've not met her yet' … response by jockey Carl Llewellyn to the pre-2005 Cheltenham Festival question, 'What will be your best ride of the week?'

'At least I already have the guarantee of three votes from my mum and two sisters' … quite why Welsh jockey Sam Thomas, nominated as most eligible bachelor in *Company* magazine's poll, thought his mum and sisters would regard him as such is a mystery. *Racing Post, 3 May 2005*

SHAKEN UP
'The practice of pumping a horse's stomach full of a bicarbonate wash, which reduces his ability to produce lactic acid and therefore enables him to run flat out for longer; Paul Haigh on a practice apparently widespread in the States, called Milkshaking. *Racing Post, 25 May 2005*

SHAKE-OUT
'There's a shake-out coming. No doubt about it. When it comes, those courses who have been thinking about the future will do

well' … and, unsurprisingly, Lord Hesketh reckons that one of those forward-thinking venues will be his own Huntingdon. *Telegraph, 3 November 2005*

SHAKESPEARE WAS A RACING MAN AND A PUNTER
'I would my horse had the speed of your tongue' … nice line from Shakespeare's *Much Ado About Nothing*, spoken by character Signior Benedick.
'O! for a horse with wings' … from *Cymbeline*.
'What a horse should have he did not lack, save a proud rider on so proud a back' … from *Venus and Adonis*.
'A horse! A horse! My kingdom for a horse' … *Richard III*.
'I will lay odds, that ere the yeere expire, we beare our Civill Swords' … first attested use of 'oddes' in a betting context, from *Henry IV*.

SHERGAR
'You'll need a telescope to see the rest' radio commentator Peter Bromley, shouting home Shergar in the 1981 Derby.

SHIT HAPPENS
'Believe it or not, most people who watch racing like a bet and don't give a shit about all the sentimental crap that goes with it' … that's *Weekender* journalist Tom Segal's December 2004 opinion, anyway.

'**That first ride at Newton Abbot scared the shit out of me and I decided there and then that there had to be better ways of earning a living**' ... jockey Jean-Pierre Guillambert on his rapid, early-career decision to switch from the jumps to the Flat. *The Sportsman, 21 September 2006*

SHOULDERS
'**You don't really rub shoulders with them, do you? You pick up your saddle, you go into the enclosure and you saddle up. The only person who has come up to me is Sir Mark Prescott. He's a great chap**' ... trainer Pam Sly asked what it was like 'rubbing shoulders' with the 'big boys' after her 10000 Guineas triumph with Speciosa in 2006

SHOWER
'**The jockeys have said I'm more than welcome to shower in their changing rooms, but I turned the offer down**' ... female jockey in Bahrain, Charlotte Kerton, who did not take up the kind offer, bemoaning the lack of facilities for her at Sakhir racecourse. *Racing World, March 2006*

SHY
'**Suffers so badly from shyness that he once famously fled across the Longchamp paddock in order to avoid the attentions of a TV crew**' ... Paul Haigh on trainer Jonathan Pearse. *Racing Post, 20 July 2005*

SIBLING RIVALRY

'All I do for a living is show off while my brother is a real genius'
... Clare Balding, having just won the Broadcaster of the Year Award
at the 2004 Horse Race Writers & Photographers' Lunch, reveals
what her granny thinks of her.

SICK

**'One drink-crazed racegoer managed to get into the weighing room
and was promptly 'Moby Dick' all over the racecourse announcer's
equipment. He received a police caution'** ... Claude Duval on York's
2005 Ebor meeting. *The Sun, August 2005*

**'It leaves a sick taste in the mouth. It is a huge blow – all the
horses I had got used to and the staff, all gone. We have been told
we might restart in 18 months'** ... English trainer Nigel Smith in
Beijing where a purpose-built equine centre and racetrack, opened in
August 2002, funded by Hong Kong tycoon YP Cheng, hoping to
take advantage of more liberal rules on gambling there, was
suddenly scrapped in November 2005 on the eve of the richest
meeting of the season. Subsequently a reported 400 racehorses and
mares were 'culled.'

SILENCE

**'I will never forget the silence of the Yorkshire crowd after this
race for as long as I live'** ... pro gambler Dave Nevison who had just
watched his 'biggest ever single bet' almost landed by Glistening in

the 2006 Ebor only to be thwarted, along with most of those present, by the late run of 100/1 outsider Mudawin.

SILKY SKILLS

'My racing silks are made of Japanese silk, not nylon like most. They cost an absolute fortune, about £400 a set and they only last about four washes. But the silk ones are my lucky set; when I put them on I feel as though I am flying' ... Frankie Dettori, interviewed by Steve King in October 2005.

SILVER

'I'm rather pleased it's a glass thing. We used to win all those silver trophies, but we only had the one daily woman, and you just can't clean them all.' ... trainer Henry Cecil on the angst we must all feel when picking up yet another piece of silver for the study. His Star Cluster had just won at Sandown in July 2006.

SIMPLY ...

'The Arlington Million doesn't pretend to be a world championship race. It pretends to be the best day's turf racing in America, a self-sufficient precursor of the Breeders Cup; and it is all of that' ... Paul Haigh. *Racing Post, 13 August 2005*

SIZE DOESN'T MATTER

'Athleticism, alacrity and balance count for more in a steeple-chaser than size' ... Marten Julian. *Racing Post, 5 December 2004*

SKINNY

'Skinny dwarfs whose leaders are paid better than the greatest statesmen' ... not a contemporary rant about waif-like supermodels, no one J Runciman, author of *Ethics of the Turf's* opinion of jockeys – in 1889.

SKIRTS

'I can't help thinking a lot of unnecessary bets have been placed by people just because they like short skirts' ... odd, but logical enough, reasoning by 76-year-old John Greetham whose Oaks contender Short Skirt was a springer in the 2006 market for the race.

SKULDUGGERY

'I'm worried that the betting ring has become an open door to money-laundering and organised crime. There's evidence of the Russian mafia working its way in. I've been told I'd better watch it because I was taking about people who would stop at nothing' ... former Tory Party leader, Iain Duncan Smith's warning as he studied the on-course betting system. *News of the World, 3 February 2005*

'There is another leading jockey who I will no longer back when he is on a well supported horse in a popular handicap. And I know a lot of people think the same as me. Skulduggery has always been part of the game, perhaps part of its appeal, but it seems to have got out of hand' ... Jonathan Rendall, *The Times, 4 December 2004*

'I am very sad to hear 70% of those surveyed think it's fixed. I go racing every day and I can say it is certainly not fixed' ... said Derek Thompson on 10 December in 2004. It was in response to a poll of over 1,000 listeners of the station for which he regularly broadcast, talkSPORT, which resulted in 70% of respondents voting 'yes' to the question: 'Do you believe that horseracing is a corrupt sport?'. 16% were 'don't knows' and 14% said 'No'.

'Racing thrives on an element of skulduggery' ... Merrick Francis, son of Dick. *Weekender, 3 September 2005.*

'Whenever anyone asks me I always say that what goes on in my books is far worse than in the racing world. Now I am beginning to wonder' ... Dick Francis, who says he was only once asked to stop a horse, a favourite at Bangor trained by his brother Doug. They were offered £50 each but 'told him to go to hell'. *Mail on Sunday, 27 August 2006*

SLOGAN
'Where the past is unique history and the future an unpredictable mystery' ... Barbados Turf Club, which celebrated its centenary of administering and promoting the island's racing in 2005.
'Setting the pace' ... Market Rasen racecourse.
'The home of racing' ... Newmarket racecourse.
'We're still unappealing, but we're not as unappealing as tuberculosis' ... *Racing Post* scribe Peter Thomas offers the betting shop industry a slogan it is unlikely to adopt on 16 December 2004.

SMELL
'I don't ride and I hate horses – they smell from both ends – but I love racing' ... which explains why 34 year old Tim Rogers married 30 year old Julie Burn at Cheltenham racecourse on 27 July 1996.

SMILE
'It's like the Cheltenham Festival, but with a smile on its face' ... trainer Ted Walsh's description of the Punchestown equivalent.
Evening Standard, 27 April 2005

'Big race days without Frankie's pizzazz are definitely missing something, even if we did see Mick Kinane smile for probably the first time in 15 years when, turning 46, he became the Royal Ascot champion' ... Robin Oakley on a Royal meeting without both Ascot – it was run at York – and the suspended champion jockey. *Spectator* 25 June 2005 Kinane greeted his triumph by commenting: 'The older you get the more you have to prove yourself.'

SNAKE VENOM
'I've admitted having the syringe, the snake venom, and that I intended to use it, but at the time I didn't know I was committing an offence' ... not a sentence you'd read every day in the *Racing Post*. This one appeared on 2 March 2006, attributed to Grand National winning jockey turned trainer Nigel Hawke. The venom is believed to be useful in stemming bleeding.

SOFTIES
'**When Scobie Breasley, now 90 and still going strong, won his second Lincoln at Doncaster on Riot Act in 1966 there were 49 runners. Are we getting soft?**' ... Claude Duval reporting that the Lincoln field maximum is down to 22. *The Sun, 2 April 2005*

SOMEWHERE ELSE
'**I don't want to be here – I'd rather be at the sales buying Contraband**' ... so Martin Pipe nipped out of the cinema where he had been taken against his will to watch the movie *Seabiscuit*, and arranged to buy the horse which, on 15 March, won the Arkle Trophy at the 2005 Cheltenham Festival.

SORRY?
'**It's terrific for the Festival and a real feather in the racecourse's cap**' ... it is difficult to see how the visit to Cheltenham by the Mongolian ambassador, Dailrain Davaasambuu to see Ulaan Baatar, named after that country's capital but with whom he had no other link, could really benefit anyone! But Jane Blunden, author of *The Definitive Guide To Mongolia*, had a different opinion. *Racing Post, 6 March 2005* .

'**The colours will be correct but two horses will be carrying number eight saddlecloths**' ... baffling course announcement prior to the first race at Leopardstown on 27 December 2005.

S.P.

'Why should the prices in Ladbrokes be the same as the prices in Coral? If Tesco and Sainsbury's agreed a common pricing system on a small range of products, the competition authorities would quickly dismantle it' ... David Ashforth asks a pertinent question about the starting price system. *Racing Post, 4 August 2005*

SPEED

'It wasn't just the speed I was doing – the fellow couldn't believe that I was old enough to drive' ... new champion jockey Jamie Spencer recalling being stopped for driving at 'about 120' on his way to Brighton for his first ride in England at the age of 19. *Guardian, 8 November 2005*

SPIT

'If anyone ever had a right to turn around and spit on horse racing, it was me, I can tell you. But the reason I didn't is that I've loved all the people and I've had a lot of fun' ... ensconced in his 14th yard, trainer Rod Simpson recalled setbacks including owners who were arrested, one who hanged himself, another who went bust, and a job in Dubai from which 'I didn't walk away from it. I ran.' *Guardian, 15 October 2006*

SPIVS AND TOFFS

'Horse racing has always been a sport supported by a mixture of toffs and spivs' ... and one wonders in which camp Greg Dyke would place himself. *The Independent, 23 May 2005*

SPOILED

'Looking back, I think I was massively spoiled at Godolphin' ...
Jeremy Noseda on his 18 month spell which didn't really work out
for him. *Guardian, 9 September 2006.*

SPONSORED WALKS

'The horses that I back don't race, they go for sponsored walks' ...
Kevin G A Smith, Chairman of The Racing Club of Ireland, quoted in
2002's *The Sweeney Guide to the Irish Turf.*

SPONSORS

**'Racing in France struggles to attract sponsors, largely because
racing is often not considered a sport, but merely an offshoot of
the gambling industry by many potential benefactors'** ... Desmond
Stoneham, French racing expert for the *Racing Post*, in July 2006.

STABLES

'I've been in every stable bar the one in Bethlehem' ... rookie
trainer Mick Murphy, who has been around a bit, celebrates his
debut winner Ballymartin Star, triumphant in a Tralee bumper on 23
August 2005.

STALLS

**'We find it totally unacceptable that the number of injuries
sustained by horses and the continued risk taken by stalls
handlers and jockeys can be viewed as acceptable'** ... July 2005
letter to the *Racing Post* by sixteen leading trainers and six top

jockeys, including John Gosden, Mick Channon, Michael Stoute, Frankie Dettori and Kevin Darley, complaining about the recently introduced Steriline starting stalls.

STARVING
'He kept all his rivals out of the handicap, and I did enjoy it, seeing all those other jockeys starving to do the weight' ... trainer Francois Doumen recalling the heyday of his great staying hurdler, Baracouda. *Racing Post, 10 November 2005*

STAYING ALIVE
'Any horse can go fast for a mile, but can they do it for two miles' ... trainer Hugh Morrison wonders why there is no staying race at the Breeders Cup, October 2005.

'Honoured Sir, your horse can stay four miles, but takes a hell of a long time to do it' ... triple Grand National winning jockey turned top flat trainer, Tom Olliver, must have been one of, if not the, first to put a pushy owner in his place with this comment, made shortly before his death in 1874.

STEEPLECHASING
'Steeplechasing, once so popular a form of sport, now appears to have seen its best days. Now that casts-off from Flat racing are put to jumping and races are held over 'made' courses with regulation fences, steeplechasing seems to have lost much of its popularity' ... W A C Blew in his 1900 book, *Racing*.

STEERING

'**Egan is one of those jockeys people like to entrust to do the steering when the money is down**' ... writer Eddie Fremantle on jockey John Egan. *The Observer, 8 October 2006*

STETSON

'**In the lounge bar, three elderly Guinness drinkers are gawping silently at the Racing Channel. One of them, it should be noted, is wearing his best suit, sandals and a Stetson hat striped in the national colours of green, white and gold**' ... broadcaster Danny Kelly, on holiday in his native Ireland, observes racing fans in their habitat of 'one of those twilit pubs that appear unaltered since the 1920s.' *The Times, 4 September 2006*

STEWARDS

'**The idea that decisions involving potentially huge amounts of money can be made by non-accountable members of an exclusive private club, populated by tweed-suited chinless wonders and ladies who lunch, is ridiculous in the modern world**' ... anti-steward rant by pro gambler Dave Nevison who did at least admit that it was provoked by news that an original decision to void a race which had cost him 'the lion's share of a big rollover jackpot', had been reversed. *Racing & Football Outlook, 29 March-4 April 2005*

'**I thought I might put them above the bed, but there might be a stewards enquiry from my wife**' ... racegoer Rob Phillips who had just paid £870 at auction to buy the 'L Dettori and AP McCoy' jockey boards in a sale of Ascot memorabilia.

'**From the experience I have had with them (stewards) over the years I think that when the door is closed they reach a lot of their verdicts by picking straws!**' … John Francome. *Born Lucky, 1985.*

'**I think the main reason I spent so much time in the Stewards' Room was that they quite rightly detected and resented the fact that I rarely took them seriously**' … John Francome. *Born Lucky, 1985.*

STILTS
'**Short of raising the entire edifice onto 12ft high stilts, or removing an equivalent depth of soil from beneath every yard of the track it is hard to see how any amount of work will make much difference**' … Greg Wood on the disastrous lack of viewing at the new Ascot, adding, damningly, 'Ascot used to have an air of effortless supremacy and class about it but it seems to be vanishing in front of our eyes.' *Guardian, 22 August 2006*

STINKER
'**He rode a stinker and I'm fed up**' … unusually harsh criticism of a jockey by a trainer – Criquette Head-Maarek decides she has had enough of Olivier Peslier's riding after her Quiet Royal was beaten in the 2006 Prix Maurice de Gheest at Deauville. 'I've had enough,' she added, 'and the problem is a clash of personalities between Peslier and myself.'

'His stinker here can be put down more to the rider's apparent longing to get back to the dryness of the weighing room in an unrealistically quick time' ... *Racing Post* race analysis in early July 2007 after Paul Mulrennan's ride on Copernican at Lingfield for Sir Mark Prescott saw the horse ridden along too quickly too early.

STOCKING TOP
'She is the equine equivalent of the woman with a hat over one eye, a cigarette holder and revolver in her stocking top' ... Richard Edmondson getting a little over-excited describing French filly, Shawanda. *The Independent, 14 September 2005*

STREAK
'It was disgusting and spoilt a beautiful day out – the group he was with were taking bets as to whether he would streak or not. They had something like £140 in the kitty to pay the fine' ... Racegoer Kathy Kinsella was shocked when 29-year-old barman Stephen Brighton, from, er, Littlehampton, stripped off and raced on to the course at Fontwell on 8 May 1995 – only to be promptly walloped by Richard Dunwoody's whip, then knocked over by Boxing Match, ridden by Rodney Farrant. Brighton was arrested and lived to tell the tale. Boxing Match's close up in the *Racing Post* read 'prominent, weakening when hit streaker after 7th, pulled up.'

STRICTLY FOR THE BIRDS
'Seagulls are a protected species and frequently inhabit Sandown,

but the prevalence of birds on Wednesday far exceeded the usual number.' ... Melbourne Racing Club chief executive Warren Brown after five jockeys were unseated after a flock of seagulls flew towards the field during a race, later voided, at the Club's Sandown track on 30 March 2005.

STRUGGLE
'About the best thing in racing is when two good horses single themselves out from the rest of the field and have a long, drawn-out struggle' ... George Lambton from his 1924 autobiography, *Man and Horses I Have Known*. He was thinking back to Ard Patrick's 1903 Eclipse defeat of Sceptre but the principle is still relevant.

STUNG
'Having been stung plenty of times before, your literature has convinced me to try once again. Here's hoping that you make us plenty of money' ... letter from an anonymous Ipswich punter who had also sent £90 to an exposed bogus tipster, 'Michael Davenport'. proving that you can fool some of the people all of the time. *Daily Mirror, 16 March 2006*

STUPID
'I was never going to be a jockey and I am far too stupid to do anything else. But I am not daft enough to think I got the job for any other reason than my name' ... Ed – son of John – Dunlop, trainer of Ouija Board. *Daily Mail, 13 June 2005*

STUPIDITY

'Their stupidity can only be marvelled at: they were willing to risk £53,946 for a potential gain of £54, although they believed their risk to be nil, since Kicking King had been withdraw from the race' ... Mike Atherton is incredulous that nine layers on the betting exchanges offered 999/1 about Kicking King winning the 2005 Cheltenham Gold Cup following an injury scare which saw even his trainer Tom Taaffe announce that there was almost no chance of the horse taking part. He did, and won as 7/2 favourite.

SUBSTITUTE

'If you're a substitute like yer man here, it's like bringing on Jurgen Klinsmann. I backed him at 25/1 to pay for the shampoo and I suppose I'll have to buy a pair of slippers' ... owner of 2006 Grand National winner Numbersixvalverde (the address of his Portuguese holiday home) Bernard Carroll on stand-in rider Niall 'Slippers' his dad is known as Boots, his younger brother, 'Socks' Madden.

SUCCESS

'Godolphin is inextricably linked to Dubai; ergo success is imperative' ... Julian Muscat on Sheikh Mohammed's need for Godolphin to flourish. *The Times, 4 October 2005*

'Niall Quinn bred her but she has been a lot more successful than Sunderland' ... Tony Newcombe after Gaelic Princess won at Salisbury on 31 August 2006 – when Sunderland were languishing at the foot of the Championship after acting manager Niall Quinn resigned in favour of Roy Keane, to concentrate on being chairman of the club.

SUCKER
'Easy talk could have led to easy money and another little sucker would have been in the web' ... Brough Scott recalls the time in November 1969 when he turned down a £500 offer to go easy on a mount at Windsor. Watchman finished 7th but 'promise, he was 'off' for his life'. *Racing Post, 18 July 2006*

SUFFRAGETTE
'Sad accident caused through the abominable conduct of brutal lunatic woman' ... description by Queen Mary of the actions of suffragette Emily Wilding Davison, who threw herself under King George V's horse, Anmer in the Derby of 4 June 1913, injuring jockey Herbert Jones and causing her own death.

SUICIDE
'It's important always to have at least one ante-post betting slip. It helps put you off suicide and means that when you die, at least you've left something' ... David Ashforth. *Racing Post, 7 July 2005*

SUN
'The sun always seems to be shining at the racetrack when Dettori is around' ... Hugh McIlvanney. *Sunday Times, 10 September 2006*

SUNDAY BEST?

'The situation exists because of the greed of the wealthiest people in racing, the big bookies, at the primary expense of the poorest – those who have to work to put the show on the road' … John Francome is no fan of Sunday racing. *The Sun, 4 December 2004*

'To have racing on Easter Sunday seems to me symptomatic of the direction in which this country is heading. It shows a complete disregard for one of the most important days in the calendar. How long will it be before we are racing on Christmas Day?' … trainer David Loder appears to believe that press gangs will arrive to drag those to the races who might otherwise prefer not to go on certain days. *The Sportsman, 15 April 2006*

'Sunday racing leaves me completely cold' … Nicky Henderson. *The Sportsman, 15 April 2006*

'Many very good people in England think it is a shocking thing that the French should run races on a Sunday, and still more shocking that Englishmen should join in what is so very dreadful' … *Bell's Life* newspaper, *18 April 1847.*

SUPERFICIAL

'The reason Royal Ascot gets a huge audience is, yes, it's top class racing, but why, suddenly, do another million and a half people tune in? To watch the people. Racing may think that is superficial but, in terms of television, it's great viewing. Racing, unlike other

sports, has the ability to cross over' ... Clare Balding. *Racing Post, 22 June 2006*

SUPERSTITIOUS
'I'm not superstitious, but I have this thing with black cats. When I was walking Point Given from the barn to the track, a black cat bolted in front of us. I froze. We were the favourite and finished fifth' ... trainer Bob Baffert on his 2001 Kentucky Derby loser, proving that, yes, he is in fact superstitious, after all!

SURELY SOME MISTAKE?
'We came, we saw and we drank, but we didn't conquer. We didn't vici, but we did veni and vidi and we definitely did vino as well' ... so much so, perhaps, that Nicky Henderson convinced himself that he and the owners of Geos, beaten in the Prix la Barka at Auteuil, were actually in Italy, or Ancient Rome, on 29 May 2005, rather than France.

SWEEPING STATEMENT
'The owner has named Light On The Broom after me because I don't like to sweep up the yard' ... trainer Gerry Stack on his May 2005 Down Royal chase winner.

SWEET
'(Luca) Cumani knows that keeping the women in his life sweet with a nice horse to ride is much better value than a shopping trip to Gucci and he gets a win percentage for his trouble' ... former

trainer David Loder explains why the Italian handler seems to like to set his wife Sara or daughter Francesca up with a fancied runner in ladies' races. *The Sportsman, 8 July 2006*

SWIMMING
'**English men wear long swimming shorts. In Europe we wear tight fitted trunks. You need to wise up and get rid of those things. They are not flattering**' ... unexpected advice from Frankie Dettori in October 2005

SYSTEM WORKING, SEND MORE MONEY
'**In each race, note the shortest priced course and distance winner and the one bet for the day is the one at the shortest price**' ... Cheltenham scheme suggested by *Racing Ahead's* 'Fenman' in March 2005.

TAKE YOUR PICK
'**If someone said to me, "you can pick, win the Guineas, or become champion jockey", I'd pick being champion. Maybe in ten years' time that will change**' ... newly crowned 2006 champion Flat jockey, Ryan Moore, 23. *Sunday Times, 22 October 2006*

TAKING THE ...
'**They are made to wait as long as twenty minutes for one race, during which time two riders jump off to urinate in the trees**' ... Nick Godfrey on a race meeting at the Royal Turf Club, Nanglerng, Thailand. *Racing Post, 10 April 2005*

TALENT
'Top horses may owe their success to an unscrupulous veterinarian as well as their own innate talent' ... Paul Haigh's investigation into American racing's 'spiralling drug problem' in May 2005 made for uncomfortable reading.

TALK DOWN
'Racing doesn't help itself, with its near-compulsion to talk horses down rather than up' ... Laura Thompson. *Racing Post, 2 October 2006*

TAPES
'When I started we were not allowed to say a word until the tapes went up, and we had to stop 50 yards short of the finishing-line in case we confused the judge' ... 90-year-old former racecourse commentator, Cloudesley Marsham, who started at Market Rasen in 1956. *The Sun, 10 February 2007*

TAXI
'I did renew my taxi driver's licence before I came out here. Now I'll be able to get a new taxi' ... Aussie trainer Joe Janiak as his raider Takeover Target to won the 2006 Royal Ascot King's Stand Stakes.

TEARS
'When you take that first step on the racetrack and they start playing 'My Old Kentucky Home' you're going to get tears in your

eyes. It's happened to me every time I've ridden in the Derby' …
veteran US jock Bill Shoemaker in 1985 to then rookie rider Gary
Stevens. *Sunday Independent, May 2005*

TELLYTUBBIES
'I've written to Eastenders to complain about how we are
portrayed. We're thugs, money launderers and drug dealers. It's a
travesty. They can't even count on TV, I saw a £100 bet at 50/1
paid out as £5,000. What happened to the £100 stake money?
They are clueless' … Anita Graham, 2004 Betting Shop Manager of
the Year is not pleased with some media portrayal of bookies.

'There are times when his colleagues are made to feel like Dr
Watson on a bad day' … Ian Carnaby on Channel 4 and *Timeform's*
Jim McGrath, adding that he is 'the man most likely to influence the
destination of an attentive punter's final shilling.'

'Sadly, racing hardly attracts the younger viewer. Therefore it is
not particularly attractive to advertisers' … David Kerr, Channel 4
head of sport as the broadcaster mused over whether to continue
showing the races. *Daily Mail, 10 December 2004*

THAT'LL TEACH 'EM
'Horses got the better of me in the end and I gave up teaching for
them' … former school mistress, Henrietta Knight. *Observer Sports
Monthly, March 2005*

THAT'S WRITE

'Always more Jilly Cooper than Norman Mailer' ... critic Jackie Dineen on John Francome's novels. *Pacemaker, December 2004*

'It's the sort of book your mother, who knows little about racing, would think you would like as a present. Try to look pleased if you receive a copy' ... what you might call damning with faint praise in reviewer Sam Kempe's *Pacemaker* comments about Anne Holland's *Best Mate: The Illustrated Story* book.

'The Jimmy White of racing journalism' ... TV racing pundit Mike Cattermole on *The Independent* racing writer Richard Edmondson who does not, as far as I am aware, harbour thoughts of being runner-up in the Snooker World Championship.

THERAPY

'The Roy Keane of racing, an Irish jump jockey so single-minded in pursuit of winners it is a wonder some educated eejit has not referred him for addiction therapy' ... *Daily Telegraph* columnist Mick Hume, railing against anti-gamblers and bigging up Tony McCoy. *The Telegraph, 17 March 2006*

THEY DO THINGS DIFFERENT

'In the US, a punter is not charged the earth to view the Breeders' Cup, and the amenities mean that the customer is very much the king. Hand on heart, can anyone who has paid through the nose

on a British racecourse, claim the same?' ... Gary Selby.
Pacemaker, December 2004

'In theory, the French mutuel betting system is better, but in practice it's the British system that comes out on top. Too much money escapes from the kitty in France. And in England each racecourse is independent. I'm sorry to say it, but I think we get a much better welcome from British racecourses than the English would get from us' ... Anglophile French trainer Guillaume Macaire.
Racing Review, March 2002

THINK
'Horses don't think, which is why it's so difficult for us to understand them' ... mind you, it isn't always that easy to comprehend what David Ashforth is on about. *Racing Post, 11 May 2005*

'He could even think like a horse' ... jump jockey Graham Bradley on his childhood hero, Lester Piggott. *The Observer, May 2001*

'That's one thing about not wanting to talk very much – I get time to read about racing, and to listen and to think' ... the always taciturn Lester Piggott, interviewed in 1970 by Kenneth Harris.

THOROUGHBREDS
'Thoroughbreds for me are about speed and not about how well you can jump' ... Rishi Persad on why he prefers Flat to jumps.
Racing Ahead, August 2005

'The thoroughbred remains the supreme example of how improvement in performance can be maintained over many generations and leaves a parallel evolution of talent of various kinds in human as a tantalising might-have-been' ... Peter Willett. *Pacemaker, July 2006*

THREE IN A ROW
'I think it's outrageous that a horse runs three days in a row' ... RSPCA equine consultant is not happy as Martin Pipe sends out Commercial Flyer for a third outing in as many days as he bids to win the trainer's title in April 2005.

THRILL
'The thrill of victory was decidedly less than I anticipated. That led me to do a lot of soul-searching' ... top US jockey Pat Day, having spent time alone in a Kentucky cabin, considering his future after hip surgery, announcing his retirement. *Sunday Independent, 15 August 2005*

'If I could win the Kentucky Derby, there would be nothing on the face of the earth, other than the birth of my son 14 years ago to compare with the thrill and the high of it' ... former pop star David Cassidy whose Mayan King was aimed at the 2006 Kentucky Derby.

TIME
'If you give time to a big two year old you can end up with a good four year old rather than a bad two year old' ... trainer Hughie

Morrison preaches the virtues of patience. *Racing Post, 17 August 2007*

TIPPING

'I don't think Desert Orchid is going to win today – and don't rule out Norton's Coin' ... said Richard Pitman to John Inverdale, who invested 'a fiver' on the 100/1 no-hoper who duly won the 1990 Cheltenham Gold Cup. *Daily Telegraph, 18 March 2005*

'If it's female, aged four years or older and is trained by Sir Michael Stoute, back it every time it runs' ... RP *Weekender* columnist Mark Blackman. March 2005

'Listening to Richard Edmondson of *The Independent* telling me what might win' ... bizarre 'favourite recreation' listing in *Cricketers' Who's Who* by umpire Ian Gould.

'I am not the snappiest dresser on the track but if someone comes up with a tip, I just look at their shoes. If they are wearing a £250 pair of Church's I might pay attention' ... pro punter Dave Nevison. *The Telegraph, 16 June 2005*

'The trainer said quite plainly that if I wanted information about his runners I should "put a f**king horse with him"' ... David Buik of Cantor on the time he took an anonymous trainer of a Sandown runner to task for inaccurate guidance about the prospects of a runner he talked down just before it romped home. *Inside Edge, September 2004*

'We're running them because we think they're well. We don't need to be a tipping service' ... Sir Michael Stoute. *The Observer, 30 July 2006*

TIPSTER
'In my day we had Gully Gully, who dressed up in a black cloak as a wizard. He would have an apple in his mitts and suddenly it would disappear and come back cut in half with a tip in it' ... Core! Veteran bookie Sammy Nixon, in his 80th year, remembers the good old days. *Inside Edge, January 2005.*

'It could have been a lot better, and would have been, if it wasn't for Pricewise' ... William Hill chief executive David Harding 'credits' the *Racing Post* tipster's ten week winning streak of big race tips for denting his company's profits. *Racing Post, 5 September 2005*

TOILET
'At Ayr you are never far from a toilet. If you drank all week, you still wouldn't be able to use all of them' ... David Ashforth on Ayr's facilities. *Racing Post, 19 September 2005*

TONGUE IN CHEEK
'I stick my tongue in my cheek and wind them up. When they ask you bloody silly questions you tell them absolute crap and they take you seriously' ... Ginger McCain. *Racing Post, 12 February 2006*

TON UP
'Every year we keep telling ourselves that it is not the important

thing to get 100 winners, but it probably is really, and now I'd be
disappointed if I didn't get it'** ... Mark Johnston on 29 August
2005, having just chalked up a 12th consecutive century of winners
for the season.

TOPLESS
**'Knowing the old Essex foghorn, who started betting at Romford
dogs in 1968 it would not surprise me if topless girls were hired
as his settlers'** ... *The Sun*'s Claude Duval on the opening of high
profile bookie Barry Dennis' first betting shop in Romford in August
2005. *The Sun, 20 August 2005*

TOPPER
'I've got plenty of flat caps but I ain't got a topper' ... Wetherby
trainer Robin Bastiman revealing that he hoped to have his first
Royal Ascot runner in 2006

TOP SHELF
**'I don't buy books off the top shelf and my book ain't a top-
shelf book'** ... Jenny Pitman on why she fell out with ghost writer of
her novels, Peter Burden, although she did also remark, 'I love
romance, I love passion, believe it or not I still like sex'. *Racing Post,
1 September 2006.*

TORTURE
**'I don't like to travel far to my racing – if you lose, a two hour
return journey is torture'** ... actor, owner, gambler Omar Sharif.
Sports Adviser

TRACTOR
'I am really only the tractor driver these days' … veteran trainer
Robin Bastiman self-deprecatingly deflects the praise to son and
daughter Harvey and Rebecca after landing his biggest success with
Borderlescott in the 2006 Stewards Cup.

TRAINER
**'In the paddock we might talk about how pretty the girl next door
is, but that's about it, because if I ever try to give him instructions
he'll ask me just how many winners I rode'** … Nigel Twiston-Davies
knows his role in the relationship with stable jockey Carl Llewellyn.
The Festival, March 2005

'I know for a fact he's got some pretty awful horses to win a race'
… Carl Llewellyn's tribute to his guvnor, Nigel Twiston-Davies. *The
Festival, March 2005*

'You were bloody hopeless' … trainer Jack Waugh assessing young
George Duffield after his first winner, Syllable, at Yarmouth in 1967.
Yet Duffield would dedicate his autobiography *Gentleman George* to
Waugh: 'the man to whom I owe everything.'

**'I run a training stable, not a hotel. If a horse is not able to run
and win money, I will inform the owner immediately and move the
animal on'** … got that? French trainer Joel Boisnard's attitude,
explained to Jocelyn de Moubray. *Pacemaker, May 2005*

'I'll be guided by my trainer – she will ask my advice and then tell me what to do' ... Brian Kearney, owner of Moscow Flyer, on trainer Jessica Harington. *Racing Post, 17 March 2005*

'The bespectacled beanpole they call The Skeleton' ... Cornelius Lysaght on James Fanshawe.

'His eccentricities, including giving his horses unpronounceable Persian names, transcended his lack of success and made him one of racing's great characters' ... racing anorak John Randall on the late trainer, John Meacock, amongst whose charges were Vakil-ul-Mulka and Qalibashi. Julian Wilson wrote of Meacock: 'He wore a battered trilby, smoked incessantly through a cigarette holder, scattering ash indiscriminately, wrote unintelligible poetry and was quite the dottiest man I ever met.'

'I'd be honoured to be half as good' ... up and coming trainer Lawney Hill on being compared to Henrietta Knight in September 2005.

'Some trainers, particularly on the Flat, react to the most benign questions as if you had just asked for their unmarried daughter's mobile phone number' ... Alastair Down's December, 2005 observation reminded me of the time a few years back when I rang a trainer to ask him politely whether his horse was an intended runner in a race my company was sponsoring – 'Don't you ****ing know I've just got out of the ****ing bath to answer this call?' he demanded. Before refusing to answer the question.

'Knowing something no one else knows' … the enigmatic Barney Curley, asked the secret of success for a trainer after his Bold Phoenix won at Wolverhampton in February 2006

'Too many people forget that he reinvented how to train a racehorse' … Tony McCoy on his former mentor, Martin Pipe. *The Times, 28 April 2006*

'Racehorses become what the trainer makes of them' … James Bethell on what he learned from former boss Arthur Budgett. *Racing Post, 27 July 2006*

'The good trainer studies the mind of his animal; the bad trainer doesn't know his own mind' … 1945 racing wisdom from writer John Betts.

'Horses are my one and only hobby or weakness. From the day they are born they become one of the family and my wife and I watch them grow and hope to see one of them make its name' … homespun philosophy from early 1960s, Leicester-based trainer S J H Carver.

TRAIN-ER
'Stan Moore, the only trainer called after a London Underground station' … Sir Clement Freud. *Racing Post, 2 December 2004*

TRAINING

'If there's ever any mention of me training, there's an immediate reaction from my dad, which is "absolutely not"' ... Francesca, daughter of Luca, Cumani. *Pacemaker, May 2006*

'Depending on one's frame of mind, training racehorses might variously be described as a vocation, a livelihood, or an affliction' ... Bill O'Gorman in his *Racing Horses*.

'When Davoski gave me my first Cheltenham winner last month it was like Jonny Wilkinson kicking his World Cup drop goal or Matthew Pinsent receiving his Olympic medal' ... well, for YOU, maybe, Dr Philip Pritchard, but probably not for the rest of us. *Evening Standard, 7 December 2004*

'One of the few advantages of being a trainer past your sell-by-date is that what you've gained is experience. And unless you're a complete prat, you are then able to recognise and identify the sort of horses you've got' ... no prat, Patrick Haslam, one of the few trainers who can boast at least one winner at each of our 59 racecourses, plus 'I think I've also had winners at about six or seven tracks which are no longer there.'

'I believe a Morris Minor doing 40mph can overtake a Maserati doing 35' ... trainer Ivan Allan explaining why he hasn't owned a stopwatch for 35 years – er, no, I don't know what he meant, either. *Racing Review, December 2001*

'**I'm a big believer in leading from the top and there isn't a job in the yard I won't do if I have to, whether it's clearing the drains or mucking out**' ... Mark Pitman, no longer a trainer. *Racing Review, December 2002*

TRIBUTE

'**Sam Waley-Cohen, who rides with the initial of his late brother sewn into his saddle**' ... poignant tribute to younger sibling Thomas, who died of bone cancer aged 20, by Sam who rode Liberthine to win the 2005 Cheltenham Festival Mildmay of Flete Chase. *Racing Post, 18 March 2005*

TRIUMPH

'**After Bago's triumph in the Arc last year, Pease bought himself the full set of the *Dictionary of National Biography*, all 60 volumes of it**' ... Andrew Longmore on trainer Jonathan Pease. *Sunday Times, 23 October 2005*

TRIVIAL

'**My plans to go to Newmarket were ruined by the London bombers, and as a result I missed my first win at a grade one track as an owner, which was seriously annoying**' ... oh, so that's why the bombers hit London on 7 July 2005, was it? Professional punter Dave Nevison might wish he hadn't penned that comment in his column in *Racing & Football Outlook* of 12 July-18 July 2005, although to be fair he did add: 'As I write this the emergency services are still trying to get remains out of underground tunnels which makes my disappointment trivial in the extreme.'

TROPHIES

'The trophy presentation is the post-coital cigarette of a horse race – not the main business, but an essential part of the winding down' ... Sean Magee. *Racing Post, 28 March 2005*

'I chose the engraved brandy glasses and my wife said "Pity about the inscription, we'll now have to keep them"' ... Sir Clement Freud on his reward when his Orpen Wide won at Southwell on Thursday, 16 December 2004.

TRY

'When I was told that no one has ever done it, I thought let's try it' ... and Sergeant Cecil duly obliged, winning the Northumberland Plate, the Ebor, and, in October 2005, the Cesarewitch for Rod Millman.

TV TIMES

'For the cost of a day at Sandown Park you could probably record a whole month of Countdown, with Richard Whiteley's blazer allowance included' ... Peter Thomas discussing whether Channel 4 will remain committed to televising racing. *Racing Post, 31 March 2005*

'I remember sitting in this office in north London with bullet holes in the windows, thinking this isn't my sort of scene' ... Mike

Cattermole recalls his days as an unemployment benefit officer.
Racing Ahead, April 2005

'A race on TV is a race on TV is a race on TV. They're all the same, can't convey atmosphere, can't stir the blood, can't move the soul. Racing was never meant to be watched through the lens of a camera, which can only provide a lousy substitute for the real thing' ... Tony Morris. *Racing Post, 29 April 2005*

'The Morning Line when John McCririck is not on it' ... Kieren Fallon on his favourite TV show. *Sportsman, 19 June 2006*

UNBELIEVABLE
'We came here expecting a good afternoon – but to welcome back six winners is unbelievable' ... Paul Nicholls, after making history by becoming the first trainer in Britain to saddle six winners on the same card, when Raffaello (10/11), East Lawyer (12/1), The Luder (6/4), Almost Broke (6/1), Nippy des Mottes (2/1) and Bold Fire (4/11) all won at Wincanton on 21 January 2006. Ruby Walsh rode all of them bar 'Nippy' partnered by L Heard. There were seven races in all. Ballez was pulled up in the second. On 24 February 1979, J C William sent out eight winners at Waterford Park, West Virginia.

UNEXPECTED
'An unexpected death in the family meant my racing days were limited to two last week' ... pro punter Dave Nevison. *Racing & Football Outlook, 1-7 March 2005*

UNREMARKABLE
'My love for horses seems unremarkable to me. It is part of my blood, my soul and my history' ... Sheikh Mohammed bin Rashid Al Maktoum, head of Godolphin. *Observer Sport Monthly, May 2006*

UNPREDICTABILITY
'The great thing about English racing is its variety and therefore its unpredictability. That slightly argues against punting, but unpredictability is what sport is all about' ... former England cricket skipper, Mike Atherton, who knows about punting, having won the Scoop 6. *The Sportsman, 13 September 2006*

UNSOUND
'By almost every historical measure, the American breed is the most unsound that it has ever been. In 1959 the average thoroughbred started 33 times in is life. And now it's down to 13' ... trainer Michael Dickinson reported by Jason Zinoman. *Observer Sports Monthly, August 2006*

'The great sire lines in America have become unsound and they pass along unsoundness' ... warning by *Sports Illustrated*'s William Nack – as above.

VERBALS
'I can't remember the last time a jockey made a complaint about an owner. He's entitled to his opinion but the stewards took the view that there was nothing wrong with Hinds' ride' ... stewards secretary Phil Tuck on September 19, 1995, after jockey Gary Hinds

reported Michael Clarke for verbally abusing him about the ride he had given Clarke's wife's horse The Deaconess at Nottingham. Clarke was fined £275 by the stewards for 'improper conduct'.

WAIT
'We do not wait for things to happen, we make them happen' ... Sheikh Mohammed.

'I asked if we could wait until the Sunday to close the deal, to see if Federer won the US Open' ... pro gambler Harry Findlay on how he funded the purchase of 2006 Cheltenham Festival County Hurdle winner Desert Quest from his tennis winnings.

'If someone had told me when I started out training in England at the end of 1998 that I'd still be waiting to win my first English Classic, I think I'd have said "bloody hell, I don't want to be waiting that long"' ... Jeremy Noseda, the day before the wait ended as Sixties Icon won the 2006 St Leger.

WALLET
'Can any gentleman who has lost a wallet on the racecourse – please join the queue at the racecourse office' ... racecourse announcement at Punchestown, recalled by Graham Cunningham. *Evening Standard, 27 April 2005.*

WAR
'It's not a battle, this game, it's a war. Its endless. Whether you

won or got beat, you've just got to get up in the morning and get on with it. The show has to go on' ... Mick Channon. *Four Four Two, September 2006*

WARBLINGS
'There is a simple explanation why Henrietta Knight restricts the appearances of Best Mate. It is to limit the number of times Jim Lewis gets to sing' ... letter writer Jeremy Dore of Essex spots the truth behind Best Mate's infrequent outings and his owner's celebratory warblings. *Racing Post, 6 December 2004*

WARNED OFF
'If I put all I knew into print, half of those on the Turf stage would be warned off' ... plus ça change as Sir Loftus Bates, a major turf figure of the early 20th century on the northern circuit is quoted by chronicler of the scene, John Fairfax-Blakeborough.

WASTING
'Wasting's not much fun but maybe it's just as bad being a big fat man' ... Lester Piggott, unlikely ever to find out personally about the latter part of his comment, quoted by Hugh McIlvanney from a 1967 interview.

'Wasting all the time, you can never relax. You have road rage before you get into the car' ... Johnny Murtagh. *The Independent, 31 January 2006*

'I've paid the penalty for all the wasting over the years and all the hardship and abuse I gave to my stomach' … jockey Warren O'Connor announces his September 2006 retirement with intestinal complaint, Crohn's disease.

WATERING
'Officials responsible for watering racecourses do whatever they like. As a result, punters never know what the ground is going to be, and for that reason they're doing their money and bookmaker profits are soaring' … a trainer who knows about the vagaries of betting, Barry Hills. *Racing Post, 18 August 2006*

WATERLOO CUP
'He remembers going to the Waterloo Cup when it drew bigger crowds than the Derby, although Beryl points out he very rarely remembered coming home' … Ginger McCain's wife puts him in his place, in a Peter Thomas interview from the *Racing Post* on 10 February 2006. Ginger got his revenge by saying, 'I've had two dogs in 22 years – my old dog died a couple of months ago and I miss her like crazy. I've had one wife and I think I might miss her when she goes, but I'm not sure yet.'

WAY OF LIFE
'What I do isn't work; it's a way of life' … trainer Mick Easterby. *Racing Post, 2 April 2006*

'Being a jockey isn't a job, it isn't a career, it's a way of life' ... the retiring Richard Quinn, bowing out in July 2006 after 27 years and 2,163 British winners.

WEBSITES
'Any British racecourse should have a look at kentuckyderby.com to see how far behind the times their own websites are' ... 'Tattenham Corner' column. *The Observer, 24 April 2005*

WEDDING DAY
'Please get me to the church on time' ... was the message on the notice pinned to the back of jockey Chris Maude's silks as he went out to ride at Cheltenham on Saturday 25 January 1997 hours before rushing to the church at nearby Pitchcombe to marry Clare 'Dolly' Pegna.

'My wife got a ride on our honeymoon' ... declared Richard Dunwoody in all innocence on the Morning Line of 25 January 1997.

WEIGHT PROBLEMS
'I was booked to ride at Carlisle but couldn't face getting into the car. My body was telling me it had had enough. I felt physically ill.' ... jockey John Carroll on his sudden decision to quit after 25 years of battling against his natural weight, in May 2005.

'I know in my heart it was because he reduced too hard to ride

races and it was directly connected to pulling weight every day, heaving and throwing up' ... Christin Landrum, fiancée of US jockey James Herrell, who died suddenly in November 2005.

'Many jockeys follow the sort of dietary regimes which would set alarm bells ringing if teenage girls copied them' ... Zoey Bird. *The Sun, 15 April 2006*

WEIRD
'Weird' ... Frankie Dettori, describing how it felt to ride Scorpion to win the 2005 St Leger – for 'the opposition' Coolmore Stud. Greg Wood in the *Guardian* declared: 'It is as if Manchester United allowed Chelsea to borrow Van Nistelrooy for the afternoon.'

WELCOME
'Welcome, everybody, to the 21st century racing industry with its much trumpeted resolve to modernise its practices and start to value its work force' ... Alastair Down points out that just eight of over 650 licensed trainers and permit holders could initially be bothered to nominate staff for the annual Stud and Stable Staff Awards, presented in February 2007. *Sunday Mirror, 25 February 2007*

WHAT DID THE WAR EVER DO FOR US?
'The Derby had become, more than any other in the Calendar, a race the winner of which could be predicted by the use of intelligence. The long rein of Chance was over; the Age of Reason

had dawned. It seemed to us that things, in this respect, had taken a turn for the better in the early Twenties of this century; and, looking back, it appears now that this was perhaps the only permanent benefit the human race got out of the war of 1914' ... so, now – thanks to 1940s authors Guy Griffith and Michael Oakeshott, it can be revealed that the First World War was fought in order to make finding the winner of the Derby easier!

WHAT'S HE ON ABOUT?
'Thankfully, the carrot crunchers who steward the Zummerzet gaff had the gumption to enquire why El Vaquero had shown more improvement than a Greek female athlete after a supermarket sweep around Boots' ... Mark Winstanley explaining cogently that a stewards inquiry took place at Taunton into the improved display of a runner there. *Weekender, 1 December 2004*

'Cop a prat' ... phrase used by Aussie racing writer Peter Pierce, meaning 'to suffer interference during a race'.

WHIP
'I can't understand why so few top riders are capable of using their whip in either hand. It is a particularly vital technique on courses where there isn't a continuous running rail to keep a horse straight' ... well, John, perhaps for much the same reason that so few top footballers can kick properly with either foot. Mr Francome whips it out to criticise today's jocks. *The Sun, 4 December 2004*

'It is not as if I chased after the horse and tried to kill him. It was just frustration. I wanted to catch him' ... Timmy Murphy received a seven day ban for 'improper riding' at Plumpton on 13 December 2004, after throwing his whip at his mount, Semi Precious, after falling four out. Brough Scott commented: 'Come on folks, get a sense of proportion, they are horses, not elderly aunts.'

'The reason jockeys do it, especially in the big races is because they know they won't get punished for it. They'll have a few days off and that will be it. You cannot hit living creatures. It is unacceptable in the modern world. More races are lost because of the whip than are won' ... John McCririck hits out after Christophe Soumillon won the 2006 King George at Ascot on Hurricane Run only to be suspended for six days for excessive whip use. *Daily Express, 31 July 2006*

'Racing should be about finding the fastest horses and experienced horsemen would mostly agree that the amount of cruelty involved when a small man strikes half a ton of horse with a felt-covered whip is hugely overplayed in today's ultra-sensitive society' ... Simon Holt. *Raceform Update, 30 August 2006*

WHO ARE YOU?
'As we arrived we were introduced to Her Majesty, but I got the feeling she knew who I was. Then I shook hands with Il Presidente, who had absolutely no idea who I was or what I did for a living' ... Frankie Dettori on attending a Buckingham Palace

dinner in honour of Italy's President Ciampi. *The Times, 26 March 2005*

WHY CAN'T A WOMAN?

'Perhaps the moment they lose their claim, the trainer finds it hard to sell the concept of a woman jockey to an owner. Or is it that deep down they themselves don't really believe in women jockeys?' ... former Jockeys Association supremo Michael Caulfield wrestles with the question of why lady jockeys don't seem to 'train on'. *Racing Post, 10 July 2005*

WIFE

'In the choice of a horse and a wife, a man must please himself, ignoring the opinion and advice of friends' ... George John Whyte-Melville in his 1878 Riding Recollections.

WIMPS

'My horses are not here for fun. They are fit and hardy, not wimps and there's no hiding place for them on the gallops or the racecourse' ... Mick Channon. *Mail on Sunday, 7 August 2005*

WIND ASSISTANCE

'She had a monstrous amount of gas this afternoon' ... jockey Christopher Lemaire explains his mount Divine Proportion's victory in the Prix de la Grotte in April 2005.

WINKY

'I grew up with Winky Cocks' … silly, I know, but I just love this quote from New York-based US trainer William Turner junior, who used to hand around with Winky, son of Hall of Fame jumps trainer, W Burling Cocks.

WINNER

'I have never yet had enough on a winner' … professional punter Dave Nevison's wry comment. *Racing & Football Outlook, July 2005*

'The final race was something else. My horse looked like it was going to be caught on the line, but it just held on. I knew then that I'd won a lot of money and I've hardly slept or eaten since' … just-redundant betting shop manager Ian Carswell, 37 – maybe because he couldn't settle accurately enough, to judge by this comment – who won a record £796,706.52 from Ladbrokes in late June 2005 with a 20p e-w Lucky 63, combined with a £2.40 e-w accumulator.

'Ascot has a 'Winners' bar, an excellent idea – other than that it does not appear to be very different from the adjacent 'Losers' bar' … Sir Clement Freud. *Racing Post, 12 July 2006*

'Show someone a horserace, wait until they back their first winner, and they think they invented the game' … Jeffrey Bernard, 1987

WINNING

'I couldn't be happier. It was not about winning today, it was

about coming here and doing things right' … Aidan O'Brien may have been happy after 2000 Guineas winner George Washington managed 3rd place on his comeback from injury at Goodwood on 27 August 2006, but it is doubtful that the punters who had backed him as 5/6 favourite were quite so happy. *The Times, 28 August 2006*

'Racing is primarily about winning and place money merely serves as a consolation prize. If any one has doubts about this, let him try and sell the Derby runner-up for half the money the winner would fetch, even if the race had climaxed in a photo-finish' … Tony and Anne Sweeney, authors of *The Sweeney Guide to the Irish Turf*.

WINTER
'The fact is that most horses do well during the winter. What you are looking for are those who have made better than normal progress in that period' … advice from Sir Michael Stoute. *Daily Telegraph, April 2005*

WIZARD
'He is infinitely patient, treats all his horses as individuals and is a wizard with doubtful legs' … I'm not sure whether Patricia Smyly really wanted to suggest the trainer Fulke Walwyn's limbs were of a dubious nature in her 1979 work, *Encyclopaedia of Steeplechasing*, but she was similarly amusing when referring to late 19th century amateur jockey Dennis Thirlwell as 'a musician of delicate health' who was 'at his best on highly strung horses.'

WOMEN JOCKEYS

'Women jockeys are a pain. Jumping's a man's game. They are not built like us. Most of them are as strong as half a Disprin' ... mm, wonder whether former laddish jock, Steve Smith-Eccles, still stands by his 1988 comment.

WONDERING

'In five years' time I think people in racing will look back and wonder how they did without it' ... keep an eye out for 10 July 2010, when the prediction of Tim Ricketts of Turftrax, whose speed-sensing system was being attached to runners' saddle cloths in July 2005, will be tested.

WORK

'They must work twice as hard as the boys, and be twice as dedicated. No matter how hard the boys graft, they must double it and become both mentally and physically stronger than they are' ... Ireland's first female champion apprentice, in 2004, Cathy Gannon on how girls can compete. *Racing Post, 2 July 2006*

WORRY

'We never had a worry in the world. We never worried about the tax man, never worried about the mortgage, never worried about anything. We just really enjoyed life' ... Kieren Fallon reminisces to Donn McClean about his days sharing a flat with Charlie Swan when they were both working at Kevin Prendergast's yard. *Sunday Times, 15 October 2006*

WORST
'Probably the worst ride I've ever given a horse' … Kieren Fallon after extricating Gift Horse from an almost impossible situation to WIN the 2005 Stewards Cup.

WRONG DOING
'Be in no doubt that racing 2005-style is beset with wrong-doing. That's not the wrong going, wrong trip sort of stuff many consider part of the fun of the sport. This is the daily game of 'Spot the Non-trier' – and worse. This is full-on unadulterated corruption' … a warning from the *Racing Post* Editor, Chris Smith. (*Racing Post, 15 December 2005*

XENOPHOBIA
'It was vintage Channon, banal and risible, with a streak of xenophobia and a dash of bogus sentimentality. Still, they do say he's awfully good with dumb animals' … *Mail on Sunday* writer Patrick Collins is unsympathetic to international footballer turned trainer Mick Channon's tirade against England boss Sven Goran Erikkson after England lost a friendly 4-1 in Denmark. *Mail on Sunday, 21 August 2005*

Y FRONTS
'He had been out and bought the biggest pair of Y fronts he could find, and he had written "Carrie Ford Rules OK" on them. He said if I'd won he would have pulled them over his trousers and posed in them for the cameras' … Carrie Ford reveals that the nation had a

lucky escape after Ginger McCain outspokenly refused to believe that she could win the 2005 National on Forest Gunner. She finished fifth.

YOU BET

'A bit more than £200,000' … was how much owner Michael Tabor admitted to winning after Pat Eddery won the Stewards Cup on 2 August 1997 on his 5/1 shot, Danetime.

'I liked the names of the horses' … explained American Jeff Thomasson after winning £16,474 for £2 when he picked 25/1 shot Sea Freedom to beat 100/1 chance Mirador at Ascot in June 1996, to land a record dual forecast payout.

'I shall be able to buy the lads a new hostel' … said trainer Kim Bailey after his Master Oats won the Gold Cup to follow Alderbrook's Champion Hurdle triumph, winning him bets of a reported £1.3m on 16 March 1995.

'I always try to bet to win rather than for fun' … owner David Johnson, which might explain his 'I was very angry about it' comment when he had his account closed by the very company which sparked his punting interest when in the late 1980s they held a 'corporate bash at Longchamp on Arc day.' *Racing Review, March 2002*

'On the one hand, I don't want to lose any more money; on the other hand, I want to win some. You know the feeling' … is there a punter who doesn't? David Ashforth spells it out nicely, if slightly illogically! *Racing Post, 17 December 2004*

'Any horse that runs, unless it's odds-on, is more likely to get beaten than win' … trainer Philip Hobbs seems to believe that odds determine the actual chance of a horse winning a race. *Racing Review, December 2001*

'I'm completely confident I'll have £100 of Sir Alex Ferguson's cash in my back pocket by next May. Sir Alex and I have had this friendly bet for the past ten years now. Arsenal and United: whoever finishes higher in the Premiership. Sir Alex is definitely well up on me overall' … Frankie Dettori admits to breaking the betting ban on jockeys prior to the start of the 2005/6 Premiership season. *The Times, 13 August 2005*

YOUNG
'Owners all seem to want young trainers now. The same thing happened to Fred Winter and W A Stephenson but I can't understand why. You wouldn't pick a doctor just because he's young would you?' … Martin Pipe begins to worry that he may be past his sell-by-date. *The Times, 14 February 2006*

YOUNGEST
'I was the youngest person in the world to ride a winner – and six months younger than Lester Piggott' … rider-turned-trainer of 14-race winner Bold Illusion, Malcolm Eckley, who died on the last day

of 2005, recalled the occasion on which, aged 12 in 1949, he won on Chota-Din at a Pony Turf Club race meeting at Hawthorn Hill.

YOU WHAT!

'**The number five horse**' ... US trainer Tom Amoss, asked how to pronounce his sprinter Wrzeszcz's name. *Racing Post, 6 May 2005*

9/11

'**When you're fussing over a horse's leg and you see what's happened in America, it helps put everything into perspective**' ... trainer Nicky Henderson, October 2001.

'**The Keeneland September sale session of September 11 was postponed as buyers turned in stunned sorrow to television monitors showing smouldering horrors in Manhattan rather than stylish yearlings in the local sale ring**' ... Edward L Bowen. *Racing Review, November 2001*

15

'**Alex's ambition was to clean out the local bookmaker, not the stables**' ... Jocelyn Reavey, wife of trainer Eddie, on the short lived racing career of 15-year-old wannabe jockey, Alex 'Hurricane' Higgins. *Guardian Weekend, 16 June 2007*

30

'**This is about the 30th break Gerry has had, but it was not nearly as glamorous as falling off a horse. It's crazy for someone to break**

their leg eleven times, but there you are, he's done it again' ...
Avril Scott in resigned mood after husband Gerry, 69, former starter
and former jockey, shinned up a ladder to take down the Christmas
lights, with predictable results in early January 2007. Ironically, Scott
had waited for high winds to subside before climbing the ladder.

50

**'I'd rather see a 50/1 shot win by ten lengths than a driving finish
with several horses together at the line. We like results that make
people ask "how did that win?"'** ... bizarre statement by Britain's
senior handicapper Phil Smith at the unveiling of the weights for the
2007 Cheltenham Festival.

75

**'He told me, "I work hard every day and still cover my wife at
night – so why can't he?"'** ... veteran trainer Mick Easterby, 75, on
his first ever visit to Lingfield, sends out Gentleman's Deal to win the
valuable Winter Derby, then explains why the horse's owner, Stephen
Curtis, is happy for him to combine stud and racecourse duties.

80

'I'm not 80, I'm 18 with 62 years of experience' ... inscription on
gift to Ireland's longest serving trainer Con Collins, who died two
years later in January 2007, aged 82.

85

'Sir Douglas had 85 colourful years and he did his best to enjoy them. He once told me he had done everything in racing, except become a horse' ... Jamie Osborne on the recently deceased former trainer and jockey Doug Marks, in late June 2007.

90

'I don't even like the word "champion" – I just managed to ride more winners than anyone else in one season' ... self-effacing modesty on his 90th birthday in May 2007 from 1946/47 champion – whether he likes it or not – jump jockey, Jack Dowdeswell. *Racing Post, 27 May 2007*

100,000

'Piggott may disagree, but the public's undying reverence for his genius and his untouchable status as the greatest jockey who ever overused a whip are worth a hundred thousand dukedoms' ... Matthew Norman rejects pleas for Lester to be returned his confiscated OBE – 'he'd never shown any sincere regret for defrauding the rest of us out of millions in tax' – after the maestro suffered a heart scare. Lester himself declared that he was not interested in the return of his gong. *Evening Standard, 21 May 2005*